Turning Water into Wine

TURNING WATER INTO WINE
100 Stories of God's Hand in Life

Second Edition: May 2020

Helen Brown

Reading Stones Publishing

Copyright © Helen Brown 2020

ISBN Softcover: 978-0-6488143-2-0
         eBook: 978-0-6488143-3-7

All rights reserved. No part of this book may be reproduced or transmitted in any form or by any means, electronic, or mechanical, including photocopying, recording, or by any information storage and retrieval system without the permission in writing by the copyright owner.

Unless otherwise stated Scriptures quoted here are from the King James Version (Authorised version). First published in 1611. Quoted from the KJV Classic Reference Bible, copyright 1983 by the Zondervan Corporation. Or the World English Bible, verses sourced from Biblegateway.com

Any people depicted in stock imaginary provided by Shutterstock are models and are being used for illustration purposes only

Published by: Reading Stones Publishing
                            Helen Brown & Wendy Wood
                            www.woodwendy1982.wixsite.com/readingstones
Cover Design: Wendy Wood

First edition published 2013
This edition published 2020

For more copies contact the publisher at:

Glenburnie Homestead
212 Glenburnie Road
ROB ROY NSW 2360
Mobile: 0422 577 663
Email: hbrown19561@gmail.com

CONTENTS

1	A Bridge Too Far	9
2	A Lion	10
3	An Extra Blessing	11
4	Answered Prayer	12
5	Are You Putting It Off?	13
6	Are We There Yet?	14
7	Balancing Act	15
8	Be Prepared	16
9	Beach Walk	17
10	Bitter Waters—Exodus 15:22-27	19
11	Brother!	20
12	Breaking the Mould	21
13	Common Men	22
14	Community Support	23
15	Changes	24
16	Childlike Faith	25
17	Daily Maintenance	26
18	Dependence	27
19	Detours	28
20	Different Lives	29
21	Different Plans	30
22	Distractions	31
23	Do we really listen?	32
24	Doing the Hokey Pokey	34
25	Easter Hope	35
26	Education	36
27	Eyes Wide Open	37
28	Father Forgive Them for They Know Not What They Do	38
29	Fellowship	40
30	Flights of Fancy	41
31	Finding Ourselves	42
32	Fire	43
33	Funny	44

34	Getting to Know You	45
35	Gifts, Love and Hard Work	46
36	God—A personal Trainer	48
37	God's Grace	49
38	Growth	50
39	Growing Up or Growing Older	51
40	Hanging out the Washing	52
41	Have You Changed?	53
42	Hat Trick	54
43	Healing	55
44	Help!	56
45	Holiday Blues	57
46	Honour Badges	58
47	How Much	59
48	How soon and are you ready?	60
49	I'm Sorry	61
50	It doesn't feel like Christmas	62
51	I'll Do It My Way	63
52	Life's Journey	64
53	Listen to	66
54	Logs	67
55	Materialism	68
56	Meddling	69
57	Mission Field	70
58	My Closet	71
59	My Gardener	72
60	No! God Will Save Me	73
61	Nothing New	74
62	One Winter's Night	75
63	Parents	76
64	Peaceful Sleep	77
65	Playing Games	78
66	Powerful Lights	79
67	Pray for Strangers	80
68	Procrastination	81
69	Rainbow Beach	82

70	Respect	83
71	Retro Viewing	84
72	Surprise!	85
73	Seems Too Good to be True	87
74	Smog	88
75	Spiritual Diet	89
76	Spoilt	90
77	Targets	91
78	The Big Picture	92
79	The Church—God's Family	93
80	The Daughter and the Gate	94
81	The Parable of the Soils—Matthew 13:1-9	95
82	The Snow Storm	97
83	The Story of the Three Wells	98
84	The Unseen Guest	99
85	Tough Times	100
86	Turn on the Light	101
87	Ugly Beauty	102
88	Under Attack	103
89	Unexpected Teachers	104
90	Waiting	105
91	What Faith?	106
92	What Is?	107
93	What is a Mission Field?	108
94	What Privacy?.	109
95	Who will Go?	110
96	Why I won't ask for Healing	111
97	Works	112
98	Worship	113
99	Wise Men Seek God	114
100	Writers Block	115

1

A Bridge Too Far

My imagination is running away with itself again! In my imagination, I am crossing a bridge that I may never actually have to go near, let alone cross. In my mind, I am angry, hurt, and disappointed by someone. I tell myself that I would not be able to talk to them when they call because I could not trust myself to say what Christ wants me to say. The devil would just get in the way. I am very aware of how much evil invades me all the time and wish that God could put a hedge around me just like He did with Job.

The reality check comes and there are several things that I am reminded of. Firstly, God put the hedge around Job because he was Job. "And the LORD said unto Satan, Behold, he *is* in thine hand; but save his life.'" (Job 2:6.). I am not Job and He will deal very differently with me. Secondly, I must stop telling God what to do—He is my Creator and He can do what He likes with what He makes. "Let them praise the name of the Lord, for He commanded and they were created. He hath also stablished them for ever and ever: he hath made a decree which shall not pass." (Psalm 148:5-6.). Thirdly, it is not my task to deal with those that hurt me, that is God's work. "Dearly beloved, avenge not yourselves, but *rather* give place unto wrath: for it is written, Vengeance *is* mine; I will repay, saith the Lord." (Romans 12:19).

My imagination is a gift from God, I could not write without it, but I must also remember to give God complete control, otherwise, it controls me, and my life becomes a mess.

2

A Lion

In a quiet time, these thoughts came to me: there is a lion roaring in our society. It's called the media. Why do I call it a lion? This is because it is an instrument that is being used to destroy many of the values our ancestors upheld, values which brought about the good things we now have, and they wanted us to enjoy. How are we allowing this monster to get away with this? Do we say anything when the press reports stories incorrectly? Do we complain when they use inappropriate language in films? Do we object when they assume that everyone is not faithful in marriage, and not only that, but they make fun of those that are?

Like Daniel, (Daniel chapter 6) we are faced with the destructive forces of the lions and we must be praying that God will stop them. However, Daniel was saved because he was found to be innocent before God and the King. Can we say the same? For us to be guardians of our society, like the angel that shut the lions' mouths, we must start doing some real work.

As the saying goes: "Evil prevails . . . when good men do nothing." I concede that it is hard to know where to start when faced with such a monster; however, the best start is at the same place that Daniel started. Kneeling and praying to a God who hears all our prayers and listens to all our cries. We could also include writing to the various media groups (newspapers, television stations and companies that broadcast suspect advertising) and complain loudly when they breach such standards. Let's also commend those who uphold healthy communication with the same diligence.

3

An Extra Blessing

At a Communion Service in our church I noticed, that for people with special dietary needs, there were rice crackers and water available instead of bread and grape juice. This is normal practice for our services but on this occasion, the crackers, instead of being plain, looked like a seaweed variety. I heard the elder apologise for not buying plain ones but I thought, "Why not, this is a good reminder that Jesus not only died for us on the cross and shed His blood for us, but it also reminds me that He is and still wants us to be Fishers of Men (Matthew 4:19) and was willing to die on that cross for those that have not yet come to know Him as their saviour".

Let's not get carried away and think for one minute that I am advocating that each service should have seaweed crackers. The Bible instructs us to keep things plain and simple so that we do not take the focus away from the centre of the practice, that being, remembering what Christ did for us on the Cross. However, what one person may have considered something to apologise for, another has found expands their appreciation of that particular service.

God used a dream to get Peter to expand his thinking in Acts 10:9-22 and God has used this occasion to expand my thinking about Communion. Such is the wonderful array of methods that God will use for each of us.

4

Answered Prayer

Just as I'm about to call it a night, it's as if God opens my eyes to see a cleaning job, that really needs to be taken care of before an upcoming inspection, due the next day. I'm tired, ill and it's late, so as I get into bed, I tell God that He will need to wake me early enough to take care of it before I go to work.

I have trouble getting to sleep and even debate if I should get up and do the necessary work, remembering some advice that Billy Graham's wife gave her daughter about doing her homework at night so she would sleep better, instead of leaving it until morning.

Finally, sleep comes. Then the next thing I hear is the phone ringing. I wake, answer it, find that no one is there and as I replace the handset, I turn the light on to see what time it is, as its pitch dark. Who rings at 5.00 am? Then I remember, "Well I did ask God to wake me up".

As I do the job that I had seen the night before, and others that members of the family had failed to do after being asked, I marvel at how God's ways are not my ways (Isa 55:8) and wonder if God feels annoyed when people don't answer His call to ministry so that He has to adjust someone else's life to make sure that His will is carried out. "Jesus saith unto them, 'My meat is to do the will of him that sent me, and to finish his work. Say not ye, there are yet four months, and *then* cometh harvest? behold, I say unto you, Lift up your eyes, and look on the fields; for they are white already to harvest.'" John 4:34-35.

5

Are You Putting It Off?

As a teenager, I was climbing a steep learning curve, as some of us have to when we strike out on our own. Yes, I was broke, (well, finances were very tight), when my grandparents decided to come and visit for the weekend on their way to visit friends at the coast. Now these people I loved dearly and I wanted so much to be able to show them how grown up their grandchild was, but how could I do this at this stage? Wouldn't I be better getting them to come later when I had a better handle on the money situation and I could afford to feed them?

Even though this couple was getting on in life they were still young (only in their early 70's) and, according to all 16 of their grandchildren, they were going to live until they were 100. They seemed healthy enough to do that. The debate went around and around but somehow with prayer and support from some friends and work colleagues, it was settled that were to come and stay for the weekend.

I don't remember much about what we all did that weekend except that on the Saturday, Grandma wasn't feeling great and had decided to stay in bed for the day, so Grandpa and I got busy making a small garden out the front of the place I lived, in order to brighten it up a bit and give it a more cared-for look. At about 3.00 pm Grandpa took a break to check on his wife and I had this thought: "Yes, well, maybe they wouldn't live to the expected 100."

About two weeks passed and there was a phone call from home, during work, to tell me that Grandpa had died on top of a mountain, on the way home. It turned out that I had been the last family member to share time with him before he went home to Heaven.

2 Corinthians 6:2 reminds us that, now is the day of salvation. When will you be called? What are you putting off?

6

Are We There Yet?

During a school holiday, I was driving into town to top up our food supply. I was thinking about all those people driving long distances to holiday destinations and those with young children who were going to hear the inevitable cry "Are we there yet?" Even the Queensland Road Department has put signs on their highways telling children how far it is to the next big town or city. I guess they are hoping to provide some sort of distraction for the children rather than the drivers. I also wondered about the Israelite parents in the wilderness and how many times in the forty years that they were waiting to enter the Promised Land did that question get asked, "Are we there yet?"

I had been cleaning windows before I left, and even with the best will in the world, I was unable to get a smudge-free finish. Talking to God about this He reminded me that I was not perfect. If I was perfect then that would mean that I had arrived and as you are not in Heaven, you have not arrived. We are not there until we have reached Heaven.

Now that's not to say there is anything wrong with perfectly clean, smudge-free windows; but God does not need clean windows to see what I am doing and to live in my house with me. In fact, dirty windows remind me that we cannot see His entire plan clearly until we arrive in Heaven. Both 1 Cor 13:12 and 1 Peter 4:13 tell us that when His glory is revealed, we will be very glad. No, we are not there yet, but God wants to help us each day with His love, support, care and strength and He will use all sorts of things and people to keep reminding us that we have a long journey in front of us.

7

Balancing Act

I was part of a group listening to a gentleman recounting his experience of being helped to regain his balance, after being very ill. As he was standing with the help of the physiotherapist, another patient called out, "Look up! Look up at the ceiling." The gentleman recalled that once he took the advice he found it much easier to balance correctly.

As I listened to the story, I realised that there are many times in the Bible when people are instructed to look up. The Psalmist in Psalm 121 tells us that he lifts his eyes to the hills, and asks "where does my help come from?" Then verse 2 declares that the help comes from the Lord. Matthew 14:22-33 tells us what happened when Peter got out of the boat and walked on the water to Jesus. He did so successfully until he took his eyes off Jesus. Then he started to sink.

How important is it then for us to keep looking up at Jesus to keep our balance in a very unbalanced world? Where are you looking right now?

8

Be Prepared

The motto of the Boy Scouts and Girl Guides is "Be Prepared". In Matthew 24 & 25 God tells us to be prepared for the Second Coming of Jesus Christ and/or our journey into the eternal world. But there are also instructions to read the signs around us and be wise enough to put in place strategies that we will need to ride out what storm we can see approaching.

God in his gracefulness sometimes sees fit to warn us of upcoming storms in life. This was the case when a man heard from a shoeshine boy about the likelihood of the stock market crash and sold all his shares. I know of a family who started an annual holiday trip without their regular prayer time. When they remembered, they stopped right where they were and prayed for a safe journey. A few miles further on they came across an accident that they would have been in the middle of if they had not stopped by the roadside and prayed. God gave us brains to use and He expects us to be sensible, like the 5 virgins in Matthew 25: 1-13 who took spare oil with them.

We would not set out on any journey without a spare tyre, a map or enough petrol, but every day, people get up and set out on their daily journey and don't even invite Jesus to come with them when their journey into the eternal world could start in a split second. Jesus says in John 14:6 "Jesus saith unto him, I am the way, the truth, and the life: no man cometh unto the Father, but by me." So why don't we ask Him to be with us every day!

9

Beach Walk

Walking along a beach, I watched a father help his daughter build a sandcastle. It was almost finished, and he was digging the trench to the sea which would allow the sea to fill the moat around the castle. His daughter, in the meantime, was impatient and kept rushing to the water's edge, waving her arms about, trying to entice the sea into the trench. I had to smile, no matter how hard she tried, that water was not going to obey her. Yes, it would fill the moat in its own good time, but only when the tide was high enough to do so.

Further along the beach, a fisherman was also standing at the waterline, and when asked how he was getting on, he replied "Only fair" but we could see some fish in his bucket.

As Christians and church organizations, we can often make plans and then we try to get God to bless them or move according to our wishes. Shouldn't we be like the fisherman? He stood on the beach and fished, reaching out into the water with his fishing line, unlike the little girl, who was trying to get the water to do what she wanted. We can be fishermen for God's Kingdom, reaching out to those who need to hear of His love and Grace and watch His power at work, instead of trying to build our own constructions.

In Matthew 4, when Jesus called his disciples we read: "Come follow me," Jesus said, "and I will make you fishers of men." At once, they left their nets and followed Him." (verse 19-20). James 4:13-15 warns us not to leave the Will of God out of any plans we make.

Years ago, before all the medications we have nowadays were available, a doctor had a patient with high blood pressure who was in danger of having a heart attack. His prescription was that the patient should go to church each week. It was not because at church the man would learn about his need for Salvation, or that by going to church God would heal his high blood pressure. The doctor's prescription was based on the need for this man to stop running around, stop working so much. He needed rest. By instructing the man to go to church, the doctor was enforcing at least one hour a week of stillness in his life.

The devil is very good at convincing us that if we are rushing around, we must be effective for God but that may not be the case. We will not be effective for Him if we take our eyes off our Lord and King and trust in our works.

That's why Jesus cried "yet not as I will, but as you will", (Matthew 26:39) and why on occasions Jesus had to tell Satan to get behind Him. There is a time to work and a time to rest (Ecclesiastes 3:1-9) but it is only when we stay close to our Father that He can instruct us as to what we should be doing.

10

Bitter Waters—Exodus 15:22-27

When we read the story of Moses casting the branch into the waters to make them sweet enough for the people of Israel to drink, do you wonder what that sort of miracle would look like today?

Some years ago, a Minister and his wife left their family and took up their first ministry position in a town where the congregation consisted of pensioners and young families. One member of the church, at least, could see that the minister's wife could have a very difficult time as she tried to cope with no children at home and a new job. Realizing this, they asked the Lord to help them find some way to connect with the minister's wife, to help her through this.

Some days later that person starting writing poetry—nothing spectacular there, except that when this lady was at school, her worst subject was English and the part of English she hated the most was poetry. But there it was—one poem and then another. Why? God had made way for the connection to be made—the ministers' wife wrote poetry too.

God had turned the waters of bitter failure at school into something good enough to help someone else survive the thirst of a wilderness.

When we pray in order to help someone else, there is no way of telling how God will answer that prayer. Just like Paul says, in Ephesians 3:20 "Now unto him that is able to do exceedingly abundantly above all that we ask or think, according to the power that worketh in us,".

11

Brother!

Picture a three-year-old girl playing with her doll and an eighteen-month-old boy playing with his toys, seemingly together quite happily in a playroom while their mother works in the nearby kitchen, grabbing as much time as she can to get all the things done that have to happen before tea is ready. At some point, the mother becomes aware that there is a problem in the playroom. On investigation, she discovers that her son has kicked over her daughter's doll which was standing up against the doorjamb. "Pick up your sister's doll, please," instructs Mum. "No!" comes the reply. "Pick up your sister's doll please," Mum has another go and the son realises that mum means business. So ok! The boy picks up the doll and stands it back up against the doorjamb, except that this time the doll is standing on its head and not its feet.

How much like Jonah! This brother had to be asked more than once to do something, and then when he did do it, he made sure Mum knew that he was not happy about what was required of him.

Are there times when we react like this when God asks us to do something? We know what happened to Jonah, and we can expect that there will be consequences for us as well. Is God asking you to do something for Him that is outside your comfort zone? Maybe it's something that will require you changing a personal custom? While you may not be running away like Jonah, maybe you are rebelling against God in some other way?

12

Breaking the Mould

At a recent discussion in a Bible Study group about witnessing to family members, a group member related how as a child they were sent to assist a neighbour with some housework. The neighbour showed them how they wanted their pillowcases hung on the line. The child then went home and with great enthusiasm told her mother about a great way to hang out pillowcases. The mother's reply was that she has been trying to get pillowcases hung out in that manner for years, only the child was not listening. It took someone outside the family to get the message through!

Even Jesus knew that people do not listen to those who are familiar to them. (John 4:44). ("Now Jesus himself had pointed out that a prophet has no honour in his own country.") How hard is it for us to listen to what God has to tell us, through those people around us, who are always there? It appears that the message gets blocked, not because of what we are being told, but because of who the messenger is.

So, now that we understand the problem, it is up to us to break the mould, to be different from those around us. So, each time someone tells us something, we need to pray and ask God if He has a message for us, regardless of whom the messenger is, whether they are family members, our minister, or close friends.

As God's chosen saints we have the privilege to be able to hear exactly what we need to hear. The Holy Spirit will assist us, but first, we must ask God to help us hear what He is trying to tell us. Matthew 13:16 says, "But blessed are your eyes, for they see; and your ears, for they hear."

13

Common Men

I was surprised one day when a "nodding" acquaintance actually said hello and started a conversation, instead of just returning my nod which they usually did when we passed each other in the street.

Being reached out to was so unusual that I had to make a quick decision, pass by, or stop and chat. Chat it is — 'How are things going?' If there is one thing that I have learnt about breaking the ice in many situations, it is this: if you want people to talk, ask them to talk about themselves.

As the acquaintance tells of the family health issues and troubles it occurs to me that these things are some the great social levellers that come with life. It does not matter how much money you have made, where you live or what social standing you may have, illness and troubles will be part of your life.

I remember as I pray for this family one night that there are a couple of other levellers in life as well.

"For all have sinned, and come short of the glory of God;" (Rom 3:23).

Hebrews 9:27 "And as it is appointed for men to die once, but after this the judgment,", and John 3:16 "For God so loved the world, that he gave his only begotten Son, that whosoever believeth in him should not perish, but have everlasting life."

It's important to remember that God's love is for everyone that He has made, no matter who we think we are!

14

Community Support

I travel to Sydney from time to time and seeing heritage buildings, particularly the terrace houses, almost transports me back in time. I can nearly see children playing cricket, hopscotch, or soccer in the streets with adults chatting on their very small porches.

They say that it takes a community to raise a child but that community has to be interactive. It may be as simple as the grocer on the corner jostling little "Johnny's" hair and asking him if he has been a good boy. By being interactive, those living in bad situations can observe the better side of life and make choices to be better, greater, kinder, or happier.

The examples that are being shared with today's generation largely come from a box called a TV. The quality of the examples are decided by a few people with questionable motives "to sell," regardless of moral lessons presented. TV shows feed us a diet of "fairy tales" several times a day. The News then feeds us a dessert of doom, gloom and horror. When we see, hear and digest such a diet of information from all around the world, is it any wonder, then, that people lose sight of what is real?

When you talk to real people, you hear how God has worked in their lives and how a lot of people experience the same difficulties. We are able to realise what biased information we are being fed daily, but best of all we are able to encourage one another. Most importantly, let us be sure we know God is real, His love is genuine, His grace is available to all, His power is invincible, His justice is unsurpassed, His word is true, His promises unbreakable and He is concerned for each and every one of us.

Isaiah 9:6 says "For unto us a child is born, and his name shall be called Wonderful, Counsellor, The mighty God, The everlasting Father, The Prince of Peace."

15

Changes

During the movie "Anne of Green Gables, the Sequel" Mrs Lind comments on a letter from Anne that tells of her trip by steam train to Boston for Christmas. With a voice full of disapproval, Mrs Lind remarks that all this rushing around must be the work of the devil and will end up being a disaster for mankind.

What people of that generation would make of how fast we move and how far we go now, can be left to the imagination. But I wonder if there is an element of truth in her so-called prophecy. We know that some of the most effective tortures employed by enemy forces in history have been sleep deprivation and persistent noise. They deprive the tortured victim of time to restore their bodies and minds and therefore inhibit their ability to think straight.

One of the things that happens because we can move so quickly from place to place is that we cram more and more into our lives. (It's not time that goes by faster, it's our using it up faster).

Some years ago, it occurred to me that if the devil keeps us rushing around and sleep-deprived then he has a very effective method of keeping the human race distracted from the most important thing in this world — God's Will.

It is not without good reason that God rested on the seventh day and in Exodus 20:9 God sets it down in law — "Six days shall ye labour and do all your work but the seventh day is a Sabbath to the Lord your God. On it you shall not do any work." Psalm 4, 23 and 46 all advise us to be quiet and learn of God — we cannot be quiet without resting.

16

Childlike Faith

After a long illness, a mother is taken to hospital for an operation while her toddler is still sleeping. When the child awakes sometime later, they emerge from their bedroom and announce that "Mummy has gone to the doctor and the doctor is going to make her all better". It was a statement of faith in the doctor. It was not related to any facts. Anything could have gone wrong, from a car accident to a medical crisis during the operation and after all, the doctor was human. This child was not concerned, unlike the adults, with any of the "what if's" that surrounded the mother's operation. They were only interested in the faith that they had placed in the doctor's ability to cure their mother.

I realised that unlike this child's faith in the doctor, my faith in God my Father, Saviour and Friend could be found wanting. As an adult, I find it too easy to entertain those thoughts of "What if?" far too often. I should have the same faith in God as this child expressed in the doctor. After all, God is far greater than the doctor. When we go to Jesus for forgiveness, ".... he is faithful and righteous to forgive us the sins, and to cleanse us from all unrighteousness." (1 John 1:9) and his word tells us that He will be with us always (Joshua 1:9). Mark 10:13-16 tells us how much Jesus understood the importance of children and in Matthew 17: 14-21 we are reminded that faith does not have to be great to achieve unlimited things.

So, from now on when I am tempted to ask, "What if?" hopefully I will remember that a child has shown me what faith is.

17

Daily Maintenance

I was cleaning my windows the other day and again I was amazed at how dirty they were. How can something that isn't used every day, and doesn't have little children pressing up against it with dirty hands, get so dirty? If I was a young parent with young children, I could understand the dirt and grime but there is no such activity in this house! Yet as I cleaned, the paper towels were just covered in dirt. It was in the air and it attached itself to my windows. Again, God reminded me that if we do not do the day to day maintenance on our lives, with daily bible study and prayer, then our lives would also get covered in the grime of sin without (I suspect) us even noticing.

God instructed the Israelites to love Him with all their hearts and to teach His ways diligently to their children. I am sure that some of His people thought it was overkill when they were told to write them upon the posts of their houses and gates (Deuteronomy 6:1-9), but God knows that unless we are very diligent, there is no way that we can stay close to Him and we will soon find that we have moved away from the Spirit. Jesus knew how important the acts of praying and talking to His father were for His spiritual health. How much more do we need to do the same thing?

God again reminded me that unless I do the daily maintenance, whether it's the windows or anything else, things will deteriorate just because I didn't do anything. Our spiritual lives are the only things that will last into eternity and that's a very good reason to maintain their good health, not just every day, but every minute of the day!

18

Dependence

With a possible health problem looming I spent, to my shame, a whole weekend crying out to God, asking Him 'what I have done wrong?', asking questions about a lack of faith, and looking around me for human support that was not readily forthcoming.

When enough became enough I finally made a phone call to a long time Christian saint who has been my sounding board and constant teacher for many years.

The advice is as usual—good common sense and a good reminder that God is the one who knows how my body works and what my future in Him holds. There are also instructions to not listen to those who would strip me of my hope and faith, and Christ himself reinforced this advice with the reading on the following Sunday from Isaiah 2:22: "Stop trusting in man, whose breath is in his nostrils; for of what account is he?" God is the one who can heal if He wishes and He can even show me what to do to bring about that healing. My duty is to do what He requires of me now, have faith in His love, His care and be obedient when He shows me what He wants me to do.

Calmness is restored and I start to think properly again. I realise "Oh how the devil feeds on our feelings of hopelessness and grows our fears to the point that we are unable to stay focused on the centre of our being—Jesus Christ."

As I search the scriptures, I find Psalm 28:1-9 a great comfort and remember that The Lord is (indeed) my strength and my shield; my heart must trust in Him (verse 7) and where He leads, I will follow.

19

Detours

I had to do a delivery one morning to a place which can be reached at least two different ways. Not even being sure how to get there, as I had only been there once or twice, and being born with a very poor sense of direction, I set out praying that God would help me reach my destination.

Delivery completed, it was time to return home and we drove home on what was suggested as a shorter route. The sign indicated that our target was fifteen kilometres away, so we drove and drove and drove some more. My comment to my passenger was, "that's the longest fifteen kilometres I've ever seen", to which they agreed.

However, it did remind me of a book I had read by Leigh Hatcher, "I'm not crazy just a little unwell", in which he shares his battle with Chronic Fatigue Syndrome. He shares with his readers the journey God took him on, during that very difficult time which stretched out over a number of years. His conclusion at the end of the book was, that before he got sick he had a plan and a target to reach and in the end he had reached that target, but God had taken him on a very different route to the one that he had in mind.

As people of our modern society we so often want to go straight from A to B by the shortest possible route and if the road available is a bit twisty then we get out the bulldozers and make it straight. While the Bible often mentions that Jesus will make our paths straight, (Isaiah 26:7, Psalms 107:7, Psalms 5:8) it refers to the surface that we are walking on, not the distance that we travel. The surface that we travel will be straight because we walk with Jesus.

20

Different Lives

After having some time away, I saw how the other half lives—well, some of them anyway. Some had moved into new houses and I had to come to terms with the harsh reality that my renovations were not going to be finished anytime soon. Though I allowed myself to get miserable about this for a while, I did eventually stop moping enough to see something important: the different ways God carries out the conversion of Christians.

When some people become Christians, their circumstances are changed very quickly. It's just as if they had moved into a new house, only taken with them the things that they wanted to and disposed of everything else. But others will have their lives changed one small part at a time, just like a house that is being renovated one room at a time and over a very long period.

This, of course, does not mean that either person is misunderstood any more than the other. There will always be people who, no matter what happens, will not agree with the changes that God wants to bring about in any life. I have to remember that, regardless of how long the process and how slow the progress, in my life and my house, the plan that God has for me and my life is the one that He wants and it will be the best for me.

Paul thanks God, every time he thinks about the Christians in Philippi, that God will complete the good work that He has started in them and was confident that God would carry on until Jesus returns, (Philippians 1:6). This means that we are included with those Philippians and He will always continue to work in each of our lives regardless of how our new life in Christ begins.

21

Different Plans

Recently I learnt something that I didn't know about some of the terrace houses around Sydney. While the outsides have the same façade, they have different layouts inside. I'm reminded of how much more work went into considering what would make people feel better, that is that no one is a carbon copy of anyone else and each person has needs to feel that they are an individual.

I'm thankful that God does the same thing. He has made us as individuals. He has a unique plan for everyone's life, and He treats us all in a special way that only He knows will work for each different person.

God tells us in Psalm 139:14 that, I am wonderfully made, and in Genesis 1:26 that, I am made in his image, (an indication of how great our God must be, as each person who has ever been born, is different to anyone else ever been born).

While there are some similarities with others and Christians have things in common, it is wonderful to know that God has made and loves each of us as individuals.

Have you thanked God lately for how He has made you?

22

Distractions

During a discussion about the stained-glass windows in the church, it emerged that some people were mystified about the circle of light surrounding Jesus' head. As a child I also wondered why this was shown in paintings. Then it was explained to me that it represented the light of purity, the perfection that set Jesus apart from the rest of humanity.

The reality is, of course, people would not actually have seen this when He walked upon His earth. The Bible tells us that he was not good looking, (Isaiah 53:2) ". . . He has no good looks or majesty. When we see him, there is no beauty that we should desire him." There was nothing about His looks that would make Him stand out in a crowd. As I pondered this, I realised that it would make sense for God to have things that way. Why would God want people to be side-tracked by Jesus' good looks, women swooning, and men being jealous? Jesus was not to achieve what we now call "Pop Idol Status." It would have been a huge distraction.

God wanted people to hear what Jesus had to say, listen to Him, and learn how to have their sins washed away so that they could have not only eternal life but a relationship with Him in this life. In John 6:38 Jesus says, "For I came down from Heaven not to do my will but the will of him who sent me."

There are many distractions around today: work; sport; family; possessions; even the nice weather; or the beauty of the church windows. These can all be a problem, but God wants us to put them aside and listen to Him. Matthew 13:9 says, "He who has ears to hear, let him hear."

Are you listening or distracted?

23

Do we really listen?

I heard a story from a time when married couples had very defined roles. While the roles in the story may not be relevant to women or men today, I believe the point of the story is.

A young bride is frustrated by all the small mending jobs that need to be done around her home. Her husband is very busy with work, and as her birthday approaches, he asks her for suggestions about what she would like for her birthday. They have very little money to spare so she tells him that if he fixed the door hinges, leaking taps, and other small jobs, she would be grateful.

However, this to him appears wrong. He wants to get something flashier, and so goes out and buys a new dress. It's not expensive and it's nice and useful but it was not what she requested. Every time the door squeaks, and the dripping tap drives her crazy, she is reminded that her husband did not listen. As this behaviour continued, we have a fair idea of what happened. Eventually she learns to fix the door herself, change the washers in the taps, and finds other ways to get the jobs done. One day the husband comes home and finds that he is not needed. She has gone.

Do we listen to God? He has a plan for our lives, and sometimes that plan does not fit comfortably with us. He may be asking us to do something that we don't like. He might call on us to walk a neighbour's dog when they are sick, or witness to our boss in the workplace by being a very good employee in an unpleasant environment. We may have other dreams, sometimes telling God that what he really needs to save the world is a new program, more preachers, more money to feed the homeless, fancy videos that preach the gospel, bigger churches, the list can be endless. These things are all good, they are all useful, but they may not be what God wants. In His word He says, "And I, if I am lifted up from the earth, will draw all people to myself." (John 12:32). What God wants is simple obedience because God's message to all men is simple.

He has made us, and He knows that we will complicate things as much as possible, because we are human. One of the problems non-Christians have to overcome about the way of salvation is that they can do nothing. Jesus Christ has done it all for us, and all they have to do is accept His gift of love. Even as Christians we sometimes get this Pharisee complex, which tells us that we have to work hard, we have to have programs, protocols, traditions to name a few, in order to do God's work.

As a teenager, I remember a preacher telling the story of an Italian woman who went to her Bible every time she had a problem. She would find a similar situation in the bible and then ask God to give her the same solution. For example, one night she had unexpected visitors for dinner, and she knew that the amount of food she had available would not feed her guests. So out comes the Bible and she finds the passage where Jesus feeds the five thousand. She prays along the lines of "Jesus, you did it there, do it here". The preacher made the comment that maybe that wouldn't work in our society, and I can remember feeling a bit embarrassed by her simple faith. I ask myself now "Why?" Jesus' message is simple and all he wants from us is simple, but confident faith. Was I so embarrassed by her simple faith because I lacked confidence, or because it did not appear to be sophisticated enough? Was I more concerned with how I looked to the world than how my faith looked to God? We have, probably out of love for our Lord, cleaned up the cross that he died on, we have polished it, sanded it, stained it, made it out of smooth metals, but the reality is, that the cross Christ died on was rough, hard with splinters, in a word, simple. It was not sophisticated. So, we try to do the same with our faith, polish it, dress it up, smooth out the wrinkles, when all God wants is raw confidence that He will do what he said He can do. If we have a confident faith in Christ, we do not need to dress it up to look sophisticated. We just need to ask, act, and expect Him to deliver.

Campbell Morgan has a saying "Spiritual, Simple, Successful; Carnal, Complicated, Corrupt". Do you have a Simple Confident faith in God being able to achieve what He says or are you trying to look sophisticated with a complicated approach to getting God's work done? Remember not everyone that says "Lord, Lord" on Judgement Day will be known by God (Matthew &:21-23). Are you really listening to God, are you doing His will for you or doing the work which you think needs to be done for God?

24

Doing the Hokey Pokey

I was discussing with a work colleague a particular function that we would be holding. Halfway through asking whether they would be attending, I remembered they had a religious sect affiliation that would prevent them even considering attending it. So, the question got stopped mid-sentence and I apologised for asking and said, "Sorry, I should have realised you wouldn't be able to attend". They replied, in a short version, that their affiliation had nothing to do with why they couldn't come. "I just have another engagement", they said. "I do those things I just don't advertise it."

I realised that the church is not the only place where people pretend to have one belief in certain company and another belief in other company. What's the saying? 'You can fool some of the people some of the time but not all the people all of the time?' We need to remember that we can't fool God at any time. He knows what we believe. He knows when we have one foot in and one foot out.

There will also be a day when it won't matter which foot is in or which foot is out because both feet will be firmly planted in front of God for judgement day (Hebrews 9:27. "Just as man is destined to die once, and after that to face judgment,") and he will reveal exactly what we believe and there will be no time to change our minds. Matthew 3:12 says "His winnowing fork is in his hand, and he will thoroughly cleanse his threshing floor. He will gather his wheat into the barn, but the chaff he will burn up with unquenchable fire."

We cannot be both wheat and chaff; we must be one or the other. Which are you?

25

Easter Hope

On a visit to the hospital one Good Friday we found the staff very busy, as more and more cases came in to be treated. As a nurse rushed in and out again, they commented on how they hated Easter because they get so busy. "Other people see it as a break, but we get run off our feet," they exclaimed. I nod in sympathy and acknowledge that Police Officers would feel exactly the same. Why? Because all they see is the misery of Easter — people being sick, hurt, dying, and behaving badly — is it any wonder they dread such public holidays? It would be hard for them to focus on what most of the general population do, the good things they enjoy during holiday times.

The point is, if we as Christians left our focus on this sad side of Easter, namely Good Friday, (there are plenty of groups that finish the Easter story at this point in history), we would also be in a hopeless state. Paul explains to us in 1 Corinthians 15:12-34 why things would be hopeless if Jesus did not rise from the dead. We would be facing the thought that death is the end, not being resurrected to eternal life.

This is the hope of Easter. If we accept this gift of Christ dying for us out of love and beating death to rise again, then we will be raised with all believers, raised with Christ when He returns. That is because Christ was able to beat death itself at the first Easter Time. 1 Corinthians 15:51-58.

26

Education

A study on Depression and Farmers started a debate with myself about ways we can educate people about this issue and any other issue in life. All the theory in the world is of no use unless it is put into practice. The conclusion I came to is that experience is the best form of education.

Faith in God, unless it is experienced, (James 2:17) will only grow while it is being practised. Putting old heads on young shoulders, as the saying goes, can only be done as they experience life and learn the lessons within their social climate. Even if people could learn without experience, social customs change very rapidly, and life is completely different for each person. There is a saying: God has no grandchildren, only children and this is true of learning. Only theories can be passed on, but the actual learning can only be done by the person, in the circumstances in which they stand.

Members of the church must also understand this principle when it comes to how we structure our organisations. While the pastoral care of each member needs to be taken into consideration, life around us is changing and while it will be harder for us to remain in the world but not of the world, (Romans 12:2) and still meet the needs of those around us, we cannot carry forward the lifestyles of those already gone before us. Would they want us to do things their way? They know that the message of Christ has to be given to the world as it is today, not yesterday or a hundred years ago. That was their job and in most cases, they did it very well.

Are we looking to the past, or at Jesus when trying to tell others about Him?

27

Eyes Wide Open

Prayer is something that Jesus did a lot of, in order to renew His strength. He instructs us to be in constant prayer. In Matthew 6:5-7 we are given instructions to set ourselves apart and pray to our Father in secret. God sees the heart. He knows, when we are praying, if we are just making a show or if we might be using it as a means to avoid doing what really needs to be done, like the women who always insisted on praying after dinner, leaving the rest of the family always with the washing up.

While it is a very good practice to go away somewhere quiet and focus on our prayers to our Heavenly Father, there are times when it is very dangerous. In Nehemiah, we read about a time Nehemiah prays to his God in Heaven in the very presence of King Artaxerxes. (Nehemiah 2:1-4). Now let's just imagine what would have happened if Nehemiah had closed his eyes to pray to his God right there in front of the King. As it was, Nehemiah was on shaky ground because he was looking sad. Had he closed his eyes to pray he would have most likely lost his head.

In modern times, there was the mother who prayed with her children at the bus stop each morning before they went to school, only one morning she was running late and closed her eyes to pray while driving to the bus stop and tipped the car over. There was another young boy who needed to pray while riding his bike and closed his eyes, crashing into a gutter.

Prayer is an essential line of communication between us and our Lord. It is our lifeline and we should continually use it but there are times when we should pray with eyes wide open.

28

Father Forgive Them for They Know Not What They Do. — Luke 23:34

A young mum with two very small children chooses to attend our traditional service, rather than the contemporary one run for those who prefer it; and, as is bound to happen, both children start crying at the same time.

I see an involuntary frown by another congregant member, and it opens the flood gates of memories of another church and another time where the same reaction happened to my children. I want to tell my story so people will understand what can happen. In the early hours of the morning, I struggle with the feelings of anger and frustration that have resurfaced. God tells me that I must deal with these before I write. He loves those in my past and those here and now that hurt me. He is still watching the children who have moved away from Him. I pray that God will help me forgive them and ask Him to take away the anger. Peace settles over me and I ask for guidance as to what to say.

There are two passages that God has given me right from the beginning of this challenge. Mark 10:14-16 "Suffer the little children to come unto me . . ." and Romans 10:14 "How then shall they call on him in whom they have not believed? and how shall they believe in him of whom they have not heard? and how shall they hear without a preacher?"

It was suggested that I choose not to bring my children to church, that I take them out. Some suggested that we attend the contemporary service, considered more suitable for small children rather than the traditional service. These are not the choices God wants us to have to make. He wants us to make choices of loving care, support, tolerance, and encouragement.

Many years ago, God validated my stubborn refusal not to take my children out of church when one Sunday I was sitting behind another mother whose young son was colouring in, and a now retired minister was preaching on Mosses and the burning bush. Without looking up the boy said to his mum, "That would be very strange". I knew then that as long as children were in church, even if they were quietly doing some other activity, they would hear His word and that meant that someday they may be able to believe.

So, I encourage all young mums, regardless of what type of service you choose to attend, keep up the struggle and I understand that it is a struggle, for the good of your children and the future of the church because they will be tomorrow's leaders.

29

Fellowship

The workday has been long and I'm feeling brain dead, it's time to go home. A co-worker asks a question that would need some explanation, so I suggest a cuppa and we all sit down for a chat. As I leave for home, I realise that the brain has revived, and the exhaustion has lifted a little. Why? The chat had resulted in a short time of fellowship about work. This reminded me of other times when I have felt the weariness of living but after having a time of fellowship with someone, either face to face or over the phone, I have felt the fatigue lift. Some years ago, we decided to celebrate New Year's Eve with friends, and we sat around talking until the TV was turned on to see the fireworks at midnight. I suddenly felt tired, but up until then, the fellowship had kept me refreshed. I remembered that a Jockey accepting the Melbourne Cup once said that the fellowship was one of the things that he enjoyed most.

So, Lord, why all these memories? They are to remind me that we are born social creatures. God has made us to have fellowship with one another. Whether it is at church, work, or sport, we are made to enjoy camaraderie with others. Genesis 2:18 says "And the Lord God said, It is not good that the man should be alone;...." While sin has largely destroyed the fellowship that should happen between a man and his wife (divorce would not exist otherwise) the need is still there to be fulfilled by others. In 1 John 1: 3-4 John tells us that we need to talk to each other in order to have good fellowship, not only at a human level but also with God as the trinity.

So, let's not neglect this necessity!

30

Flights of Fancy

One day, I was stunned to be told by a church member that they would not invite non-Christians to a special Service because it would put too much pressure on them.

At 4.30 in the morning, I was thinking about this and talking to God along these lines. Is this because they are ashamed of our preachers? This does not make sense — they would invite them to attend a program that costs money but not to a free service. Is church really only for Christians now? It never used to be! In the past, before there were programs, God managed to convict people of their sin and save them.

Then I went into fantasy mode! Something I do now and again. Lord wouldn't it be great if other members of the church just managed to invite those non-Christians anyway. Wouldn't it be even better if the message was so great that they and the whole congregation were convicted of sin and really felt the presence of the Holy Spirit at the service? But would members of the congregation publicly pray with them? It's not a thing that this church does. Lord, what would be even better is if a small child came up and said, "I'm naughty and I want Jesus to live in me and teach me how to be good." Oh yes, I could also imagine the congregation saying, "Oh that's so cute" and laughing and saying comments like "They have no idea what they are doing."

But you know what — I laid there and thanked God for reminding me of just how simple it is to come to Him and be saved. He reminded me of Mark 10:14-15 "Allow the little children to come to me! Don't forbid them, for God's Kingdom belongs to such as these. [15] Most certainly I tell you, whoever will not receive God's Kingdom like a little child, he will in no way enter into it."

Oh why, oh why do we make it so hard for people and ourselves?

31

Finding Ourselves

On yet another car trip with work colleagues, we were discussing the decline in the moral and social standards of our society. This brought to mind the advertisement about a farmer trying to find his free-range cattle in the outback. There was no fencing, so the cattle had got lost. All he could find was an artificial beast made out of a 44-gallon drum and oil can. The advertisers want us to accept as true that the production of "Free Range Cattle" will make them better in taste and quality. Now you can believe what you like but I find it hard to be convinced that I will notice any difference, personally. By taking down so many of our social/moral fences we have allowed ourselves to become a "free-range" society but what has been achieved — a better society? Or has our society just become lost like those cattle?

Proverbs 22:6 tells us that what we teach our child when they are young is what they will continue to do when they are old. If we want society to return to the times of high moral standards, then it is important that we start putting up those high moral and social fences again. A Christian revival, started by reaching out to society and telling them what God requires and how much He loves us, is the only way that those fences can be reinstated. Then society will be found. Isaiah 3:22 & 4:1 assures us that if we return to the Lord as a country, He will forgive us.

32

Fire

I read a story a long time ago about a lady in America whose house had been destroyed by a bush fire. When she examined the ruins, she was astonished to find that the houses either side of her home had been left untouched. "Why, God?" was her cry! God's question to her was "Do you love these things more than Me?"

God has been challenging me in much the same way. Would I be willing to give up all my ambitions, desires, and dreams if He requested it? I find myself attaching conditions, instead of freely letting go and letting God have control. In other words, my heart and head are in different places of acceptance.

God has the right to ask us to give up anything that He wants without giving us a reason or an outcome, other than faith in His faithfulness. He asked Abraham to give up his one and only heir. (Genesis 22:1-18). The problem I also come up with is that, unlike Abraham, I find that I would like a guarantee that the results would be the same for me as they were for Abraham. Now I'm not Abraham and God may not want to give me the same outcome. Searching my heart and scripture, I find a lack of the courage that Paul had when he set his face towards to Jerusalem. (Romans 20:22).

I also realise that many Christians are being challenged in much the same way every day. Our job as part of the family of God is to support each and every one of these family members in prayer even when we have no idea who they are. 1 Peter 4:7 says, "But the end of all things is near, therefore be clear-minded and self-controlled so that you can pray."

33

Funny

It's funny how God uses small things to make us think about the more important issues in our lives. During a big baking day, I went to put the first finished product in the fridge and discovered that there was not enough room for it to go straight in. I'm surprised at how fast the thought occurred, "I need a bigger fridge", but next, there was this now familiar tapping on my shoulder. Hang on, all you need to do is rearrange the fridge and throw out some of that rubbish.

This made me think about my life's journey. Our lives will always be on the move with many twists and turns. Those corners do seem to get closer together as we grow older. When we get around a bend we are faced with a set of different challenges and circumstances, meaning that we again have to re-evaluate some of the things that we do.

So, each time we turn a corner, do we just try to jam more and more into our lives or do we sit down and ask God to show us what needs to be rearranged, put in storage, or thrown out? Yes, these challenges will sometimes be daunting and make us feel as though we are never going to reach a point where we can cope. I imagine that Joshua could have felt overwhelmed when God asked him to take over the leadership of Israel after the death of Moses and in Joshua 1:6 God says, "Be strong and courageous." And in verse seven He says the same thing again but adds "Be careful to observe to do according to all the law which Moses my servant commanded you. Don't turn from it to the right hand or to the left, that you may have good success wherever you go." God has given us the tools to move forward and when we reach the next bend then we start all over again in His strength.

34

Getting to Know You

Here in Australia, we get a lot of news from all over the world. There was a time when there were a lot of stories about the Royal Family in Great Britain and her personal life, giving us some insight into her daily life. It got me thinking: "How would I get to know the Queen?" If I were invited to attend a Queens' Garden Party or a function and got to say hello, or invited to attend the palace for a personal encounter, could I claim to know the Queen? The only people who have some claim to this are the people who interact with her daily and get to see her when her public face is not necessary.

As members of the church, I sometimes feel that we have settled for formal gatherings, which allow us to keep up the public appearances that we would like to present. Even in small groups, it is easier because we are only together for short periods of time, it's easy to say and do what we think is expected of us. How do we get to know each other? My experience has been that it is the small things that people say in unguarded moments that reveal more about what people really think or feel. So, it would appear to me that getting to know people is more likely to happen in informal situations where they feel comfortable enough to put away their public face.

We all know that many people can read their Bible from cover to cover several times and yet because they have not let Christ into the inner parts of their lives, they cannot claim to have a personal relationship with Him. Therefore, they will miss out of the reward that God has in store for those that have got to know Him personally.

Jesus tells us in John 10:14 that he knows His sheep and His sheep know Him. Matthew 25:31-46, the parable of the Sheep and Goats, explains the difference between those who know Christ and those who Christ will disown because they haven't known Him.

Are you letting Christ know you?

35

Gifts, love, and Hard Work

John 3:16 tells us that "For God so loved the world, (you) that he gave his one and only Son, that whoever (you) believes in him should not perish, but have eternal life." The most important gift that God gave us was His son Jesus. He sent Him into our world from perfect Heaven to bridge that gap and bring us closer again.

When I was younger, I overheard some older ladies talking about how love is hard work and the example they gave was "love is changing dirty nappies". Love is hard work, we work hard at cleaning, earning money to pay the bills so our loved ones don't go hungry, playing with our children when we would rather be crashed out in bed early, teaching them good manners, thinking and praying about what is best for their welfare. These are all gifts that we give our loved ones. Since sin came into our world it has created a great gap between us and God and we no longer enjoy that close relationship with God that Adam had to start with. Having lost touch with God, we forget that God has feelings. When we throw His goodness back at Him, He hurts. When we ignore His gifts, He is disappointed, but when we accept His gifts gladly, He is lifted too.

There are three responses to gifts.

Firstly, — it can get thrown back in your face. It's not considered good enough, not liked or not what was wanted. When this happens most of us want to throw our hands in the air and say, "why do I bother?" What about the gifts that God gives us? Too much rain, not enough rain, winter is too cold, summer too hot, and soils are too heavy or too light. Does God throw His hands in the air and say, "why do I bother?"

Secondly, gifts can be ignored or get a blasé response. They can be accepted without a thank you and put aside leaving you with the feeling that your hard work is unappreciated. God also gives us all the same gifts. He sends rain to everyone and He sent Jesus to save all of us. Is our response just as blasé? So, what, I'll take whatever happens and ignore the giver?

The Third response is one that says thank you so much and that was so good of you. One year I knew that I had purchased the right gift because my child had responded with great glee and I had received the biggest hug ever. Some people will respond to God's gifts in the same way.

Jesus' saving sacrifice is a gift that is offered to each of us equally and if we think that His offering of that gift was not hard work for God—think again!

When my son was a young boy, he was a kid who wouldn't venture away from home unless he had to. It wasn't something that I pushed too much until it was time for him to go to school. Then it was a case of he had to go! As we were 'bushies' he had to get to school by getting on a bus. As a result of his unwillingness to go to school, I had to physically pick him up and put him on the bus. He was crying and I was dying inside but it had to be done. Now, I was putting my child on a bus, where, as far as I knew, he would be safely driven to school. I was also sending him to school, where, as far as I knew, he was going to learn mostly good things and be safe.

God was putting His son into a world knowing that firstly He would be born in a stable. His son, a King, born in a stable! Herod was going to try and kill Him before He was two years old, people were going to laugh at Him and He would die, inescapably, on a cross. If this was not enough—even after He was back in Heaven with His father the world would continue to mock Him and hurt Him.

How much harder was it for God to put His son into this world than it was for me to put my child on that bus? God did send Jesus because God so loved the world (you) that He gave His only begotten son so that whoever (you) believes in Him will have eternal life. What is your response to God's gift? Not good enough? I should be able to get to Heaven without Jesus? I don't care — I'll take whatever happens? Or are you wrapping your arms around the cross, thanking God that He cared enough to send Jesus to live and die on that cross for you so that you could have eternal life?

36

God—A Personal Trainer

There is a line of thinking both in the secular world and Christian circles that people should concentrate on their gifts. Let other people do what you are not very good at. While this line of thinking makes perfect sense in that we cannot do everything; other people need to be able to contribute to the success of any project; others will learn and many hands make light work, still, God is interested in us as a whole person.

In Matthew 22:37 we are instructed to love the Lord our God with all our heart, soul and mind reminding us that God is interested in our whole selves. It does not make sense that if God wanted us to worship Him with everything that we have, He would not want to make sure that every aspect of our spiritual lives is in tip-top condition.

So, while the gifts that we have are very important to Him, so are the weaker aspects of our lives. They are important because they will, when strengthened, enhance our gifts and enable us to give God greater honour. So while we are going through difficulties or just times where we do not seem to be using our obvious gifts, take it all on board because God may be just taking the time to expand those weaker areas of our lives to develop us into people with a better overall fitness than we had before. That way, in hindsight, we will know the truth of Romans 8:28 "We know that all things work together for good for those who love God, for those who are called according to his purpose.".

37

God's Grace

Flying to Sydney after a difficult week at work, I looked out of the window not long after take-off at a very thick bank of clouds. They looked like a solid layer of cotton wool. As I looked beyond the clouds to the west I could see the orange/yellow glow of a clear sky sunset.

As I looked, I realised that I was witnessing an aspect of God's beautiful creation that I would not have been able to see from the ground. I had to be lifted on the wings of the aircraft, above the clouds, to see this.

It seemed to me that the Lord had lifted me on spiritual wings to see His amazing hand at work, during the previous week, when the dark clouds of evil were very evident.

I had searched my heart and asked God to make sure that the right thing was done; not what I wanted; not what I thought was right; not what I would have liked; but His will to be made clear to all those involved and He certainly did, one step at a time.

Each day He told of the next step to take that would, as far as possible, protect me and the organisation for which I worked.

Amos 5:14 says "Seek good, and not evil, that ye may live: and so the Lord, the God of hosts, shall be with you, as ye have spoken." and oh how He has proved that to me. As we move into the future, I pray that I will remember His goodness in this situation and be reminded that He will prove it again in different ways as I step out in faith and see His handiwork.

Are you prepared to step out in faith too?

38

Growth

Some five years ago, I had to embark on a trip which involved getting into an aeroplane for the first time ever. I was so nervous that I had to ask many of my Christian friends for prayer and support. Just recently I had to take my fifth flight on an aeroplane, and I noticed that I was so much calmer this time. The difference was so marked that I wondered if God had a lesson for me to learn from the transformation.

It occurred to me that, yes, there is a lesson for all of us. As young Christians, we need to learn how to step out in faith. The first time any one of us has to step out in faith, I'm sure that we do it with fear and trembling, but God proves to be faithful to us. The next time we have to take the next step in faith we are able to step out with a little less fear and trembling. Then the next time we are able to step out with more confidence until we are able to trust God to be faithful, no matter what the circumstances and know that God will be as faithful to us as He was to Joshua, Moses, Peter, Paul and all the other Christians who have gone before us.

Our Christian life is a series of steps in faith and we should remember what the Bible tells us repeatedly, that God will be with us. See Joshua 1:9, Exodus 3:18-22, Matthew 28: 18-20, Acts 1:8 and Acts 9:15-16.

39

Growing Up or Growing Older

When reading 1 Samuel 16:1-13, about God sending Samuel to anoint a new king for Israel we get to verse 6 where Samuel is obviously impressed with the physical attributes of Jesse's eldest son; but God's response is in verse 7 is "Man looks at the outward appearance, but the Lord looks at the heart."

Oh, how we look on the outward appearances! If someone drives a nice car, they must be well off — but God knows if they own the car or the finance company does. If someone confidently presents a good resume, they must be able to do the job — only God can tell whether it is a bluff or not until they have been employed for a while. If a church is bursting at the seams, then their minister must be doing the right thing. If the numbers drop off, then he must be doing something wrong. A church is going backwards if there is not a new group being formed each week. In 2 Timothy 4:3, we read "For the time will come when they will not endure sound doctrine; but after their own lusts shall they heap to themselves teachers, having itching ears." So, having many people in a church may not mean that the preacher is preaching the word of God, but possibly only what the congregation wants to hear.

God looks on the heart of any church that is under his care and He sees the hearts of everyone who attends. He alone can tell if they are learning to grow in His grace because they are listening to a preacher speaking His Holy Word. I knew a parent once who was asked if their children were growing up. Their response was "no, just growing older." This was because they did not seem to be able to mature as children should.

Are we growing older or growing up?

40

Hanging out the Washing

A family lived in a time when the washing lines were short and pegs were expensive. So, when the washing was done it was important to be economical with both pegs and line.

One day their small daughter decided that she wanted to help, so the busy mother left her daughter to do it while she finished off other jobs.

On returning to the clothesline, Mum discovered the daughter had proudly hung all the hankies out just like a line of miniature nappies. However, this meant that each hankie had used 1.5 pegs instead of four hankies being pegged by the corner with 1 peg. The daughter had carried out the job, determined to do it her way and had not given any thought to how her mother needed the job done.

What happens when God asks us to do a job for Him? Do we charge in? Do we say we will witness for God but go ahead and do things the way we think they should be done, without asking God how He wants things carried out?

In John 8, Jesus tells the Pharisees that they were doing the work of God, but doing it their way, not the way God wanted it done. This meant that they could be condemned because they did not have a proper relationship with God. In Matthew 7:21-23 we read, "Not everyone that saith unto me, Lord, Lord, shall enter into the kingdom of heaven; but he that doeth the will of my Father which is in heaven. Many will say to me in that day, Lord, Lord, have we not prophesied in thy name? and in thy name have cast out devils? and in thy name done many wonderful works? And then will I profess unto them, I never knew you: depart from me, ye that work iniquity."

41

Have You Changed?

I met a work supervisor from a previous career of some 20 odd years ago. They commented that I had not changed one bit in that time. As the words echoed in my mind later, I thought "I hope that is only on the outside — I would hate to think that I had not changed on the inside where they cannot see."

Twenty years is a long time to not grow. Back then, I had a different career, lifestyle, and circumstances. As each of these things changed, I had to learn new skills, develop different gifts, fine-tune some of my personality traits, deal with many sins and dig deep into Christ for the strength to move forward, all of which should mean change (growth) and lots of it. During that time God has given, taken, and sent me to many places, and, if I was to remain just as I was then, there is no glorification for God in seeing me grow, and become closer to Him. Ephesians 4:14-15 reminds us that as we grow "That we henceforth be no more children, tossed to and fro, and carried about with every wind of doctrine, by the sleight of men, and cunning craftiness, whereby they lie in wait to deceive; But speaking the truth in love, may grow up into him in all things, which is the head, even Christ." And 2 Peter instructs us in Chapter 3:18 "But grow in grace, and in the knowledge of our Lord and Saviour Jesus Christ. To Him be glory both now and forever."

The outside might not have changed to look at, but I pray that the inside has changed a great deal.

42

Hat Trick

It was summertime and Cricket was the game on the TV every week. There was great excitement one weekend because one team had managed to get three batsmen out in a row, it's called a 'Hat trick'. I had this funny thought, "What would a "Hat Trick" be for a Christian Minister?" What about a funeral on a Friday, a wedding on Saturday and a baptism on the Sunday? Each one of these ceremonies represents the start of a new journey.

The funeral is the start of an eternal journey. Luke 20: 35-36 says "But those who are considered worthy of taking part in that age and in the resurrection from the dead . . . .. they can no longer die; for they are like the angels. . .... They are God's children . . ."

The wedding should be the start of a lifetime commitment, for two people. Genesis 2:24 says "Therefore a man will leave his father and his mother, and will join with his wife,. . . ." Matthew 19:6 tells us, "So that they are no more two, but one flesh. What therefore God has joined together, don't let man tear apart."

The baptism would hopefully be, in the case of infant baptism, the start of a lifetime of learning, not only the facts of Christianity, but also the experience of seeing parents living out their faith in Christ. Luke 18:15-17 is where we are told to let the little children come to Him and do not hinder them, for the kingdom of God belongs to them and Deuteronomy 6:7 instructs parents to teach Gods desires to their children, talk about them when you sit at home and when you walk along the road and when you lie down and when you get up. If we are talking about adult baptism, then the journey started should be one of living a lifetime of dedication to the work and will of God. Acts 1:5 "For John truly baptized with water; but ye shall be baptized with the Holy Ghost not many days hence."

43

Healing

On and off during my life, I have wondered about the number of miraculous healings Jesus performed while He was here on earth and why the number of healings was radically reduced after His return to Heaven.

We know that Jesus healed many more people than those recorded in the Bible and while Jesus still heals, it appears it is not in the same way or in the same number as before the ascension.

While I debated this quietly with God one night His answer came! If I had not healed so many people they could not have mocked me on the cross. This revelation puzzled me. As I continued to pray some more, I realised that this was because each one of us needed to believe that He could heal. In other words, if Jesus had healed only a few people that were actually recorded in the bible, He would not have had the reputation for being able to heal others — or being capable of healing Himself and getting down off the cross, if He wanted to. (Matthew 27:30-40). Therefore, He was able to prove to me and the rest of humanity that He really chose to die out of love for all us sinners.

John 10:11 "I am the good shepherd. The good shepherd lays down his life for the sheep."

John 11:49-50 "…"You know nothing at all, nor do you consider that it is advantageous for us that one man should die for the people, and that the whole nation not perish."

Do you appreciate that Jesus chose to die for you out of His great love?

44

Help!

O Lord, I have visitors coming and suddenly I can see dirt and dust everywhere! They're going to think I'm lazy because my windows are dirty, the furniture is broken, and the kids have left things lying around. What am I to do? The gardens a mess! There are weeds all over the place; the grass needs to be mowed. They will go away and talk about how bad I am, not to my face, of course, but tomorrow when I can't hear. I have been in their houses and they are as neat as a pin, as they say. Help me, Lord!

Firstly, the Lord said, who do you think I am going to listen to? Your prayers for their souls or their complaints about a house where I put the dust — and yes, you do have a choice; you can have a very smart house, one that is worthy of a housekeeping magazine; but have you considered the cost?

How many people will not hear that I love them because missionaries and churches will not be able to do as much as they can because of fewer funds? I know you don't think it's much but how many children will not know that I love them because scripture and Sunday school teachers are short. You will have less time to talk to me, and be tired, stressed; your back and feet will hurt all the time and your family? Will they be able to relax when they come home?

Remember what I said to Martha in Luke 10:41-42, "Martha, Martha, you are anxious and troubled about many things, but one thing is needed. Mary has chosen the good part, which will not be taken away from her."

Thank you, Lord, for the help.

45

Holiday Blues

The holiday was so refreshing; green grass, blue skies, fellowship with family and friends; but then we came home to reality; dust, dirt, and mess. I so badly wanted to create the near Heaven conditions that we had experienced while we were away. So, for three days I deliberated, planned, and strove to make it all happen. At the end of this period, depression hit with a thud because it was becoming plain that my plans were not going to come to fruition. It was then that I finally asked God what the message was that I was supposed to be getting.

Think about Jesus leaving Heaven and coming to earth, from the place of perfection to a place of sin, destruction, and struggle; and about how He will be returning someday. "Who would want to come back here, when the earth was going to be in a worse state than when He left 2000 years ago?"

Just as well He is only returning to create a new Heaven and a new earth, it would be the only way He would want to return.

John tells us in Revelation 21:1 that in his vision he saw a new Heaven and a new earth, for the first Heaven and the first earth had passed away and there was no longer any sea.

Do you look for lessons in life's events no matter how bad they are?

46

Honour Badges

One of the advertisements that I don't like is the one for "ancestry.com" in which someone talks about looking for a record of a great grandmother, finds that she had been married three times and closes with a very sarcastic comment about her popularity. It annoys me for the reason that we forget that women in ages past did not have the privileges that we have now. The social structures for women even as far back as two or three generations meant that women were not allowed to own property and many women had to have a lot of courage to marry a man in order keep a roof over their heads and that of their children. We have not walked in their shoes and I feel very sad that we cannot respect those who have had such courage in order to make sure that generations survive. They needed to rely on God so much to do some things that we would consider to be ridiculous to us today.

Exodus 20:12 says "Honour thy father and thy mother: that thy days may be long upon the land which the Lord thy God giveth thee." I have a feeling that God was not just referring to our immediate parents but also those grandparents that have loved Him and prayed in faith for your salvation even if they did not get to meet you.

Anzac Day, Remembrance Day and other Memorial Days help our generation to show respect for all those who have made great sacrifices. Let us show respect for those who have made sacrifices, even if we have no idea what they were, but without them, we would not be here today and probably would not have the lifestyle that we enjoy either, but most of all let us remember the ultimate sacrifice made by God, His Son Jesus Christ.

47

How Much?

When you do some small thing for those you care about and they don't notice, how do you feel? Ignored?

Matthew 10:5-42 tells us what Jesus had to say to his disciples before He sent them off to reach out to the Jews. Not only does He tell them some of the difficulties they would face, but He also tells them how much they are cared for.

How much do you think God cares about you? If the hairs on our heads are numbered (Matthew 10:30) and if we are known in the manner that David declares in Psalm 139, God cares about us greatly.

The next question then is, do you recognise when God does the little things that show you how much He cares for his children?

What about the time you forgot to go to a meeting only to find out later that it was cancelled, and you missed the message? Do you blame old age or thank God? Or the day that things went wrong, and circumstances put you in a different place at a different time — and you met a friend who needed to talk. Is it coincidence or God's care?

Wouldn't it be better to say thank you to God for the little things that He does rather than ignoring them, or worse still giving the credit to something else?

48

How soon and are you ready?

In Genesis, we read about the creation of the World and time and again we read "And God Said . . ." and it came into existence.

In a recent Bible study about the second coming, some people expressed reservations about what we should tell others when there appear to be a lot of things still to happen before Christ returns — do we say what the scripture says, that his return could happen at any moment when these things have not happened yet?

One of the things that life teaches those who have been around for a few years, is that when God speaks or just allows something to happen, circumstances change in a moment. Whether it is a politician's decision to change their stance on a particular policy, or an accidental event, life can change very quickly. We have seen film taken out of context and broadcasted on our TVs, and suddenly the cattle market is on shaky ground. Years ago, the wool market suffered when the floor price (a minimum price that ensured the viability of the market) was suddenly abandoned. Earthquakes have destroyed whole cities.

So how does this apply to the second coming of Christ? From Scripture in Matthew 24: 36 we read "But of that day and hour knoweth no man, no, not the angels of heaven, but my Father only." Also, in Mark 13: 32 it says, "But of that day and that hour knoweth no man, no, not the angels which are in heaven, neither the Son, but the Father." We know that God is the only one who knows when Jesus will return and the things that need to be fulfilled before then. Well, God can make them happen in a very short space of our time.

Are you ready?

49

I'm Sorry

The phone call had to be made. I realised that when, earlier in the day, a friend had rung me and poured out their troubles, I had left out some very important advice. This friend has a very difficult situation which they normally cope with quite well, however, this morning things were looking grim and a shoulder was needed. She said, "I just don't know what to do", to which I had no reply except to acknowledge that God must have made them capable or He would not have given them so much responsibility.

As I continued to pray during the day I realized that I had neglected to remind them, that God did not want them to travel this road alone. He wanted to travel it with them, and He wanted them to be dependent on Him for His strength, courage, and inspiration. He did not want them to be dependent on me or anyone else. That's not to say that I was unable to support them by praying, but the situation was one that I had no experience with.

As I prayed for forgiveness, God reminded me of the verse in Revelation 22:18-19 "If any man shall add unto these things, God shall add unto him the plagues that are written in this book: And if any man shall take away from the words of the book of this prophecy, God shall take away his part out of the book of life, and out of the holy city, and from the things which are written in this book". This was an important reminder to stay on the very straight and narrow road when it comes to telling others about God and His love.

50

It doesn't feel like Christmas

One year, in December I realised that it didn't feel as though Christmas was close. Why, and what was missing that made it feel like Christmas in the past? I'm thinking it's because we are too politically correct to sing Carols and tell the world that we are celebrating the birth of a Saviour, Christ the Lord. I have asked myself many questions. What was that first Christmas really like? How do people celebrate in places where Christmas is outlawed? How did they celebrate Christmas when even the church banned its celebration? Why do we in the southern hemisphere celebrate Christmas in summer at the busiest time of the year while our northern counterparts celebrate in the darkest time of the year? (After all, Christ was a light at the darkest time in history so far). What makes a good celebration memorable, something that our children will remember with fondness? Is it the preparations that make it feel like Christmas? What makes Christmas a magic time for Children? Isn't Christmas really about the other 364 days in the year when Christ changes our lives a little every day? How do people who are trying to cope with tragedy or bad memories feel? What about those who have to work at Christmas?

On that first Christmas, only Mary and Joseph knew that the baby she was about to give birth to was special, and maybe the wise men who may have already been following that special star, but other than these people no-one else knew anything special was about to happen. Yes, the shepherds were told after the event but not before. To the rest of the world, it was just another day with Caesar causing his usual dramas. Isaiah 55:6-7 says "Seek ye the Lord while he may be found, call ye upon him while he is near: Let the wicked forsake his way, and the unrighteous man his thoughts: and let him return unto the Lord, and he will have mercy upon him; and to our God, for he will abundantly pardon." This is the Christmas story and it should be told 365 days of the year.

51

I'll Do It My Way

I have lost count of the number of times I have asked a child to do the washing up and have been answered with "But I'd rather do the wiping up." Thinking back to a story about a man caught in a flood, telling rescuers that God would save him, I wondered how he expected God to save him. Did he expect God to transport him in the same manner that Philip was transported by the spirit after talking to the Eunuch from Ethiopia? (Acts 8:26-40). So, when we pray, do we really expect God to answer, or do we expect God to answer in accordance with our wishes. Often when you talk to people with problems, they don't really want to find out how others had solved their problems but just want answers to suit them. When solving problems, I have found that, though God's solutions were not always what I would have liked, they have worked.

Consider the Israelites and the battle with Goliath. (1 Samuel 17:25-53). They had a very real and enormous problem. All their technology was no match, without the power of God. God's solution was very simple and yes, I noted that the technology available was also used to finalize the death of the monster. A preacher once said that "Spiritual, Simple, Successful; Carnal, Complicated, Corrupt". I'm not saying that every Spiritual solution is automatically simple, but I suspect that most Carnal ones are Complicated. God's creations are never complicated; intricate, yes, but simple and so are the answers that He gives to any problem we may have. I suspect that when we make things complicated it's because we would like, in some way, to duplicate the intricate designs of God.

Do you really want God's answers?

52

Life's Journey

Recently in early May, I was driving from Inverell to Armidale to collect my husband and daughter off a flight. The route involved driving in an easterly direction, straight into the morning sun, which was blinding. There was no time to stop and wait for the sun to get higher in the sky because there were deadlines to be met. The only way forward was to slow down and keep my eyes on the white centre line that runs up the middle of the road. This got me thinking about our life's journey.

Once we repent of our sins and turn our lives around, we are moving towards Christ — the Son. Effectively we are driving into the sun. This journey will never be easy, not like driving with the sun behind you which is where we like to sun to be when we are driving.

We start off in the dark and need the headlights to guide us and so it is when we start our journey towards Christ — He provides people (ministers, Christian friends, Godly parents) to guide us as to how to live our lives differently.

But just as I was blinded by the sun and could only move forward by keeping my eyes on the centre line, often we are going to be blinded by fog, snow, rain or just the sun getting in our eyes. The only way forward for us is to keep our eyes on the word of God which is very much like that centre line in the road. There are times in our Christian journey when we feel we are only clinging by a thread and these are the times when we have to read God's Word and believe it even if it is only with our heads, leaving our hearts to catch up later. God's word will always be there, and we are always able to use it to keep us moving forward. Believe the promises of God. Joshua 1:6-7; Heb 13:5-6; John 3:16; Ps 23 & Ps 37 to name a few.

It will tell you where you are. If I had looked at that line and found it to be on my left instead of my right, (we drive on the left-hand side of the road in Australia) I would have realised that I was headed for disaster. In life, it is also possible to be heading in the right direction but driving up the wrong side of the road. Even after we have asked Christ to save us, there are times when we do not let Him be the Lord of our lives. Some people never do. If you drive on the wrong side of the road for too long, you crash and burn and so it is in life. God loves us enough to bring us to our knees and show us that we need to make the necessary corrections in life. It is still our responsibility to make sure that we listen and move over that line on to the right side of the road.

Sometimes, we will encounter snow on our journey, and this can hide even God's word. This is the most dangerous time for any Christian because it means that God's word is being covered — the Word of God being twisted to suit evil intentions. It is then that we really need to cry out to God to show us whereabouts on that road we are — on the right or the left.

To conclude I would like to ask three questions.

Firstly, are you driving in the right direction, towards the son of God and Heaven, or are you driving the easy way with God still seeing you but at your back?

Secondly, if you are driving in the right direction, which side of the road are you on? Is God the Lord of your life or are you trying to do things the way you want to?

Thirdly, when you are blinded by all the things that get in your way along your life's journey, do you remember to hang onto the word of God?

53

Listen to

Once on TV, there was a story about a man who had been taken to hospital emergency and had flatlined, meaning that he had no heartbeat! The doctors had worked on him for around 15 minutes, so they were thinking that the outcome was not going to be a good one, but before they gave up and declared the time of death, the doctor allowed that man's wife into the cubical to say her goodbyes. As she spoke to her husband, she declared her love for him and her need to continue to have him around and then, there on the screen was a pulse. The man recovered.

We know that a lot of wives so often complain about husbands not listening to them, which prompted one of the female reporters on this story to use the line "husbands listen to your wives, they may one day save your life."

But there is another voice that is desperate to save your life today. The voice of God speaks to us in many forms. Yes, He speaks to us through our husbands and wives, our friends, our ministers, history, our bodies when they are in pain or exhausted, He speaks to us through the beauty of nature, the kindness of strangers, through His word or that thought that just suddenly popped into your head. He may even stop you doing something by causing forgetfulness. God the Father, Jesus the Son and the Holy Spirit are talking to us all the time! In John 3: 16 God tells us that He loved you so much that He sent His only begotten son into the world to save your life for eternity.

Are you listening!

54

Logs

Eight millimetres, how could something that big not be seen? Let me explain, about three weeks ago, while collecting wood, I got a splinter in my finger. Poking around, I thought that I had removed it all. However, over the next week, my finger did not really get better so another attempt was made but nothing could be found. While my finger was not sore, it just didn't feel right. Then on the morning before my measuring exercise, I woke with a very sore and obviously infected finger. I thought "Maybe it's time for a doctor to fix it." Poking and prodding made my stomach lurch with pain, but I stood in the light of the window and prayed "Lord help me find this thing and stand the pain." Eventually, a very small brown speck appeared. Thinking 'that's very small to be causing so much pain', I got hold of it and started to pull. It seemed to take forever; the nerves felt each millimetre as it moved passed them.

Just like that splinter, sin can be buried, not seen, but festering below the surface of our lives. It may not even cause us a great deal of trouble, but we know that something isn't right with how we are living. God will one day bring our sins to the surface and their removal will be painful but like my finger, our lives will be so much better without them.

David knew that God could see the sins that were buried in his life (Psalm 90:8) and in Psalm 139:23 he asks God to search his heart to help him deal with any sin that needs to be removed.

As painful as it is, are we willing to stand in Gods' light and ask for His help to deal with our sins?

55

Materialism

A question about our minister not replacing his second car after it had been destroyed, triggered a conversation about how materialistic our world was now, compared to twenty years ago. Oh, how time has flown, the world is no different now to twenty years ago. Forty years ago, life was different! Wives could stay home, we could still pay the bills on a single wage and public transport was available to take us where we needed to go.

This got me thinking about the meaning of materialism and I remembered a story of a Christian lady who, throughout her life, had very few material goods and what she did have, she had to work very hard, not only to get, but to keep. Her husband died and she met and fell in love with a man who had every material comfort life could afford. The women had a real spiritual struggle. Lord! Materialism is wrong. Should she give up the man she loved because of his material wealth? God's answer was simple and direct! They are my gift to you, but I am still your Lord and I am the one to be worshipped. Enjoy the comforts that I send you but don't make them the focus of your life. They are to be used and cared for, but don't worry about scuff marks, dirt or damage.

It is not what we have, but our attitude to what we have that the Lord is interested in. We may have very little and still worship it. This is what materialism is! All the way through the Old Testament we read that our God is a Jealous God — jealous for our love. Hebrews 13:5 says, "Be free from the love of money, content with such things as you have, for he has said, "I will in no way leave you, neither will I in any way forsake you"

Who or what do you worship?

56

Meddling

I woke at 2 am, something I haven't done for quite some time. I recognised the opportunity to keep a promise to a friend and pray for them. However, this time I experienced a lot of interference. "God, you need to burn the evil out of this situation," I thought, and as I continued to try and concentrate on my prayers, I must have fallen asleep and dreamed.

It was as if I was floating over a translucent body lying on a hospital gurney and in the middle, I could see a black mass. I felt that it represented sin that is in each of us, the church, and the world. A voice was saying "Don't touch it, it can only be dealt with by a ray from up here", It was as if God was trying to tell me that His Judgment or Grace would be the most effective treatment and He could do it without any assistance from us.

As I continued to pray and think about the dream, I remembered talking to a mother some years ago about how when the doctors were carrying out a biopsy on a mass that had shown up on her son's brain, they discovered that what they were dealing with was leukaemia. They very quickly closed the incision and left it alone. They told the mother that if they had continued, it would have aggravated the cancer and made it spread faster.

God tells us that vengeance is His (Deuteronomy 32:35-36) and I remember that King David had the opportunity on two occasions to get rid of the evil (King Saul) who was damaging Israel (1 Samuel 24:1-15 and 1 Samuel 26:1-20) but he wisely left it to God to deal with.

Are we playing God or letting Him do His real work?

57

Mission Field

What do you think most children know about God? One Scripture teacher was accused of using a bad word when she told the class that she was there to teach them about God and Jesus! This is what a lot of children know about God. His name is a bad word! Most children today have no idea who created them or who made our great and wonderful world. The only way these children will find out will be if Scripture teachers continue going into our schools and telling the Bible stories that they will be able to remember later in life, to be used by God to bring them to Him. In Australia, we still have the privilege of being able to go into our schools with the message of a loving God. The other thing to remember is that our freedom to do this may be taken away from us at any time and then God will have a much harder job getting these children to hear about Him. If this mission field is ignored, these children will not know how much God loves them. How can they understand that there is a God who wants a relationship with them if someone does not tell them?

Scripture teaching is a job that many people think they cannot do, and it can be very scary to get started but it is such a very important volunteer position that really needs your assistance. If there are not enough teachers then there will be lots of adults in the future who will have a greater difficulty understanding the love of God and that He has a plan for their lives. If you cannot go into a classroom and tell children about God, then please, please pray and support those that do.

The great commission in Matthew 28:19 tells us to go into the whole world — in our town and country there is a whole world in our schools.

58

My Closet

Mathew 6:6a instructs us when you pray, go into your room, (the King James Version says "Closet") close the door and pray to your Father, who is unseen. My house is full of modern gadgets and children, which either beep at me or constantly call for my attention. My list of things to do is continually growing and when I get to work, it is more of the same except there are more machines and people; add traffic and other noises of modern living and it makes life very hectic! Where is my closet? Where can I find somewhere to do what Mary did — sit quietly at Jesus' feet (Luke 10:38-42)?

When I walk into our church, where there are very few modern technological gadgets beeping or whirring at me, I am walking into my closet — a place where I can come apart and shut out the world. I can, for one hour a week, step away from its fast pace, sit at the feet of Jesus (just like those people in the stained-glass window) and learn from Him through our hymns, Bible Readings, Prayers and what the Holy Spirit has to say through our preacher. For one hour a week, I can be Mary!

I know there will be some distractions, the traffic outside, various children climbing over seats and nearly falling off but it is still a time when I don't have the world yelling at me and I can focus on what God wants me to learn. Jesus did it and I am glad that I can do it now. Yes, I know that someday the church that stands will be obsolete and I will have to find another "closet" but right now I am very glad to have the privilege each week.

59

My Gardener

The other day as we attacked the garden yet again, I almost despaired of ever keeping my garden always looking neat and tidy. There is this stuff called rain that makes things grow and pesky things called weeds that continually need to be removed. We do this either by using chemicals, or just by persistently mowing the weeds down or pulling them out by hand. As I grumbled, I realised that a garden is always going to be a work in progress; it will always change and need to be kept under control. Just like me.

God is my gardener; He made me with a plan, made up of good things. Yes, He showers me with blessings which help the good things grow but those pesky things called sins always show their ugly heads and get in the road. God trims away at the bad stuff, sometimes using drastic methods, but mostly He just keeps reminding me of the things that I need to repent of and He helps to keep them under control; and I will always be a work in progress until I go to be with Him.

Jesus tells us in John 15:1-11 that God wants to help us grow into better people because He loves us. I will always be a work in progress, but God will do a better job with me than I will be able to do with my garden. I just don't have that much energy! But I'll look forward to my perfect garden in Heaven.

60

No! God Will Save Me

I was reminded of a story of a man clinging to a tree in a flooded river, needing to be rescued. As the story goes, men on the bank throw him a rope and he refuses, telling them that God will save him. Next, along comes a boat and he again says, "No! God will save me". Then after he has climbed to the top of the tree, a helicopter tries and he says, "No! God will save me". He drowns, dies, goes to Heaven and asks God why he didn't save him. God's reply is: "I sent you a rope, a boat and a helicopter. What more did you want?" And I think he added, "I would have helped you if you had only let me". We sometimes find ourselves clinging to a tree in a spiritual sense because we have looked around and see life as too confusing, too difficult, and too frightening and we need help.

Do we recognise what God sends to help us? The men on the bank, throwing the rope, aren't they our Christian friends who pray for us daily and share with us their experience of how God has helped them through times of trial? What of the boat? Maybe the fellowship that we share with other Christians through our Bible study groups, and our own study, that should make us think about our priorities. So, the helicopter: could that be a major life crisis that really forces us to stop what we are doing and ask God where we should be going?

In Matthew 14:22-33 the story of Jesus and Peter walking on the water reminds us that keeping our eyes on Him will enable us to live without getting swamped by the troubled waters around us.

Are you looking at what God has sent to help you or, like Peter, looking at the troubles around you?

61

Nothing New

As we celebrate 100 years of the work that John Flynn started in the outback, I'm thinking that people today are just as isolated as those people were for whom John developed the Pedal Radio. Why? Firstly, people are more mobile than ever, so best friends and family end up living a very long way away or on the other side of the world. Secondly, with families struggling to make ends meet, there is very little time left for socialising. The number of women working makes it very lonely for those women or men who choose to stay home to look after children. Thirdly, the rise in crime and antisocial behaviour makes it nearly impossible for parents to allow their children to play safely outside, and certainly makes the park experience a very scary one, even in small towns.

People go on about how dangerous social media is, particularly in relation to privacy issues. Those who are old enough to remember the party line phones will also remember that privacy has always been at risk. I find it hard to believe that some people who used the pedal radios would not have sometimes said things that they realised too late they should not have said. Social media has been blamed for many social problems and is criticized as being a weapon for evil. It appears also to be an instrument that could be useful in breaking down today's social isolation.

Ecclesiastics 1:9 tells us that there is nothing new under the sun. James 3:1-12 also tells us that the hardest part of the body to tame is the tongue, even if it is being expressed through the fingers. It's not the instrument that is evil but the way it is used. Any instrument can be used for both good and evil.

Do you use what God has allowed to be made for good or evil?

62

One Winter's Night

I sit and watch the flames burn. They wrap themselves around, through and over the pieces of wood. The warmth created spreads out into the room touching anyone near it. It occurs to me that if the Holy Spirit was the fire of God, then it would do the same to us. It would wrap itself around, through and over us. It also would touch anyone that was near enough to feel the power of God burning in those that God has chosen to be used by Him.

Again, I watch my fire and know that it burns hotter and brighter with two or three prices of wood. I'm reminded that the bible says in Matthew 18:20 "For where two or three come together in my name there am I with them."

And so, if there are more joined in the name of the Father, they will be more powerful than one alone. That's not to say that one on their own cannot be very effective for our Lord.

I watch my fire die down and know that if I am to continue to enjoy the warmth it sheds, I must soon brave the cold air outside and collect more wood. I'm also conscious that the fire of the Holy Spirit does not have to have new pieces added to it to keep it burning, but is fed by the blessing of our Lord and Saviour, to strengthen and encourage us and not destroy his precious children.

63

Parents

I was talking with my sister and in the back of my mind, there was a nagging feeling that something was really wrong with this conversation. The rest of my siblings had decided that my parents were too old to do the things that they were planning to do. Specifically, they want to hold a family reunion in July. So, my siblings were taking matters into their own hands and had planned to do something else. Now there was nothing wrong with the plan, particularly for the rest of the families involved. As far as I knew they had the financial resources to carry it out. The problem for me was that I was not in a position financially. With a young family, I was not even in a position to logistically carry out my part of the plan. As I thought, cried, and prayed about their arrangements, and tried to figure out what was wrong with the conversation, I realised that it was not the plan but the way they were treating our parents. Sure, they were getting on in years, and they had challenges to meet, but they were of a sound mind and in good health and still very capable of making their own decisions about what they wanted, should and could do. We were not in any way honouring them by making decisions for them that they were capable of making for themselves.

To resolve my mistake by taking part in the conversation in the first place, I made and sent my parents a contract, stating that while they were capable, I would allow them to do what they wanted.

One of God's commands for us in Deuteronomy 5:16 is: "Honour thy father and thy mother, as the LORD thy God hath commanded thee; that thy days may be prolonged,….."

Do we obey God in the way our parents (elderly people) are treated?

64

Peaceful Sleep

A two-year-old is experiencing fear, though we cannot see the reason — so much so that she cannot sleep in her room or venture outside at night. The parents are at a loss to understand the cause and look at the internet to find ways of trying to get rid of the negative force surrounding their child.

While discussing the issue with other Christians, it was suggested that it was a good opportunity for the parents to pray for and with, their child.

That night, at bedtime, the mother asked the child to pick a book as a bedtime story. She went hunting and found "Where is Jesus" and in it was the prayer — "Be near me Lord Jesus, I ask you to stay, Close by me forever and love me I pray." At the end of the book it closes with "I thank you for always being near me, Jesus"

That night for the first time in a long time the child slept in her bed all night.

Isaiah 50:10 says "Who is among you that feareth the Lord, that obeyeth the voice of his servant, that walketh in darkness, and hath no light? let him trust in the name of the Lord, and stay upon his God.."

Where do we go for our solutions to any situation? These days there are so many books that will tell you how to do anything; the internet can give you all sorts of information about absolutely any subject. However, there is no way of knowing how much of that information is right or wrong. There is only one source of information that has been proven to be absolutely true all the way down through history and that is the word of God. He is the one that gives Peaceful Sleep.

65

Playing Games

I was playing a computer game one day and thought that the computer was playing up, as it had been a little bit slow. I continued to blame the computer, until I realised that I was trying to play outside the rules of the game. Computer games are very unforgiving when it comes to playing by the rules.

How many times I have blamed something or someone else for things that are going wrong in my life, when all the time I was trying to play/work outside the rules set down by God? Uncountable! Yet when we become Christians there is a tendency to think that we can throw out all the rules, because after all, we are saved by grace not by the law. (Romans 6:14).

However, what God wants us to do above all else is to bring glory to Him. We are unable to do that if we are constantly breaking the rules of life. How can our God be glorified, if those who proclaim to follow him do not follow the example of Jesus? Isn't the saying "Imitation is the greatest form of flattery?" Now don't take me out of context — God does not want flattery, He demands worship!

We are told that in order to become models or witnesses to other people, we must be imitators of Christ, just as those in Thessalonica did in the time of Paul (1 Thessalonians 1:6-7). While we cannot be perfect, we must at least stop, look, think, and pray before we make decisions. That way we may have peace in our hearts about what we do.

66

Powerful Lights

On a flight to Sydney for a conference, we were coming into land at Sydney Airport in the dark. I looked out of the window and seeing the lights of Sydney brought to mind an image of thousands of strings of fairy lights strewn all over the ground. As I surveyed the view, I rejoiced in the fact that God is not watching us from a distance, but He sees each one of us as the individuals He loves, as unique creations, and His sons and daughters.

The next day at conference, I was also reminded of the picture of fairy lights when there was a reference made to some Missionaries and Christians in other places. Yes, we are like fairy lights, we are all connected to each other by the power of God's Holy Spirit, and we are to shine in all the dark places of the world. Each one of us is very small, but it is the power of God that connects us, making us all the most powerful force in the world to spread His word.

From my place in the sky, I could also see that there were places that were still dark, and so it is with those of us who are called to follow Christ. Matthew 28: 18-20 tells us that we are to go and teach all nations.

Are you shining through the power of the Holy Spirit which Jesus has offered you?

67

Pray for Strangers

The conversation was one of those that you cannot help but overhear in a public place. It broke my heart because it did not take long to realise that it was taking place between a child (around about the age of 10) and her grandfather. Why? I have heard this story many times before, but it is usually between two adults.

The child was asking her grandfather, "Why does God allow things to happen that destroy your faith and spirit?" It was obvious that this child was very disappointed in her mother's behaviour and Grandpa was trying very hard to explain to the child that life is not a free trip. Many thoughts went through my mind: this child sounds so grown up, so frustrated, very disappointed, and she is not responsible for any of these problems. My heart also went out to her grandfather who was trying so hard to be fair to all parties involved; my guess is that it was his daughter that was the child's mother and love for both people was tugging him in all directions.

I am not sure why God allowed me to overhear this conversation but I am certain that each time they are brought to mind, I need to reach out to God in prayer to heal, teach, and comfort each one of these people. It is unlikely that I will ever meet these people again, but God has also heard the conversation and will wrap His arms around each of them. Commit your works to the Lord, and your plans will be established. The Lord has made everything for its own purpose, Prov 16:3-4a.

Has God asked you to commit faithfully to something that you may never see the results of on earth? Please CONTINUE TO BE FAITHFUL; you never know who you will be helping.

68

Procrastination

Many years ago, there were two sisters living in college. There were rosters of jobs that each student had to carry out. Like many siblings, these two were very different in personality. The older was practical, the other very particular. So when it came to doing duties such as sweeping the foyer, the practical sister would grab the first broom, be it straw or whatever was available and get on with the job while the other would always spend time looking for the hair broom because that was the correct broom to use, stretching the job out unnecessarily.

Are we Spiritual procrastinators? Do we hold back from doing what God wants done because we think we need something else other than what's in front of us, or do we just get going? For instance, do we give the farmer a hand concreting even though we have our dress trousers on, or resist doing something until the right protocols are followed or the training has been done?

When we read the story of Moses and God's call to lead the people out of Egypt, we see Moses telling God time and again that he is not qualified, "Who am I that I should go to Pharaoh and bring the Israelites out of Egypt?" Exodus 3:11 and in 4: 10 "O Lord, I have never been eloquent . . . I am slow of speech and tongue."

There is a right place to use the correct tools and to have the proper training but sometimes we use these as excuses because we don't want to do what God would have us do. Often, we just need to use what God has given us just as He said to Moses in Exodus 4:2 "What is that in your hand?" and let God work the miracles.

69

Rainbow Beach

On a recent walk on Rainbow Beach, I was keeping an eye on where I was putting my bare feet, in order to avoid the dangers that lurked there (things such as sticks, jellyfish and unfortunately, needles and rubbish). I was so busy looking down that at one point I realized that I had missed seeing the majesty of the coloured sands in the cliffs. In order to see the cliffs, waves, and blue sky, I either had to stop, with my feet in a safe place and look around me or move forward in faith while looking up.

I thought, sometimes we can be so busy looking at the dangers in our world that we can miss the majesty of God and His creation, work, and power. When Peter walked on the water he looked down, saw the troubled sea and began to sink. We need to look up to see how great our God is and how much He can do. The Psalmist in Psalm 42 wonders why his soul is downcast and reminds himself of the greatness of God ". . .Therefore will I remember you.... (verse 6)

Psalm 46:10-11 says, "O my God, my soul is cast down within me: therefore will I remember thee from the land of Jordan,.."

Psalm 123:1-2 "Unto thee lift I up mine eyes, O thou that dwellest in the heavens. Behold, as the eyes of servants look unto the hand of their masters, and as the eyes of a maiden unto the hand of her mistress; so, our eyes wait upon the Lord our God, until that he have mercy upon us."

When we realize that we are too busy looking at the bad things around us, let us stop, look up and remember our wonderful God.

70

Respect

There was a weekend when several people, not just members of the family, juggled their plans and adjusted what they were doing in order to assist a couple of family members to obtain certain privileges. This would allow them to reach some outcomes, however, during this process, I became aware that they were unlikely to achieve the final goals. I moaned about the lack of respect that these people were showing to all those involved in the process and even debated if all the juggling was worth the trouble.

So, was all the trouble that Jesus went to, to die on the cross, worth it for Him? And what about the lack of respect that many of us show Him. How much respect do you show Jesus? This was a very sobering thought that followed my moaning. Jesus knew what pain He was about to endure, and He also knew how many people in the course of the history of the world would not give His pain, His gift and His love a second thought.

No wonder Jesus cried for Jerusalem (Luke 13:34) "O Jerusalem, Jerusalem, which killest the prophets, and stonest them that are sent unto thee; how often would I have gathered thy children together, as a hen doth gather her brood under her wings, and ye would not!!" He went to the cross to give His life so we could have eternal life. Yet many of us are not willing to accept everything that He has to offer. Some will accept His salvation but not His care. Others won't accept either.

Next time someone chooses to disregard a gift or effort that you have made on their behalf, remember that Jesus completely understands and made the effort anyway.

71

Retro Viewing

Watching old reruns of programs that were made thirty or forty years ago is a very good reminder of how our society thought, behaved, and generally saw the world in those days. An example is the way woman's skills were viewed in the workforce. If we are old enough to remember, it also reminds us that some things at least have changed for the better. However, we do not have to watch the news each night for very long to realise that for some people life has not changed. In some cases, things have gone backwards, and conditions are far worse than those that existed in times past.

Life will keep moving, not necessarily forward but at least round and round in circles, even if those circles are wider each time. While it looks as if things are getting better, they are only getting better for some of us and for others the world seems like a cruel and lonely place. Do you sometimes think that history is like reading different versions of the Cinderella story? — there are so many of them now, the characters are different, and the settings are different, but the storyline is still the same.

While we watch the turmoil around us and deal with the various crises that life brings our way, we can be very thankful that there is only one centre to this circle that life is on, and that centre is God the Father, Jesus Christ the Son and the Holy Spirit. God created the universe, all that is in it, including you and me. He is the one that has not changed, will not change, and cannot change. Hebrews 13:8 tells us that Christ is the same yesterday, and today and forever. That is a centre point that we are all need to hang on to.

72

Surprise!

It was a Wednesday when I had a phone call from my son. "Mum, I have missed doing a course in Inverell and the next one is on Friday in Armidale. Will you drive? It's only six hours."

What! Lord, don't you know how much I can do at home in six hours? I really wanted to mow my grass on Friday, and I need the exercise, besides, I don't know anyone over there now.

I fussed and grumbled and made myself miserable. All day, I kept asking myself, what will I do? and getting food is going to be hard. On and on I grumbled. God reminded me that I had recently spent four days doing nothing on the train. But I was going somewhere, and I really wanted to mow the grass.

Friday came and, armed with 3 books, note pad, papers for our accountant (the one job I could do in Armidale), and baked beans I set out. While driving I remembered another trip which had been very inspiring, and I almost challenged God to see if He could do the same this time around.

I dropped my son off at the required place, drove downtown, dropped papers at the accountants', then as I walked back out onto the street, I decided to take a walk up the mall to get a cuppa, and then back to the car.

I reached the corner, looked around and spotted a jewellery store that was open. I Love Jewellery . . . . and yes, I do know someone in Armidale. I wonder if that shop is the one, she owns? I'll just have a look. I wandered over and yes, it is her shop because there she is standing behind the counter. We chat and she asks what I'm doing. Killing the day, I reply. She offers to have lunch with me to help fill in the day. I arrange a time and find out where I could park all day, as the spot I was in was only for two hours.

During lunch we started talking about general things and she mentions that she was in Inverell recently for a Salvation Army conference. Suddenly, we have a very different level of conversation; we talk of Christ, church, and our walk with Him. The conversation continues well after her lunch hour is over, back at the shop.

On the way home, I realise what God has done. He has surprised me and inspired me again. As it says in James 1:17: "Every good gift and every perfect gift is from above, and cometh down from the Father of lights, with whom is no variableness, neither shadow of turning."

Will I grumble next time God asks me to do something else other than what I had planned? Probably, but hopefully I'll remember this day and wait to see what He has in store for me.

73

Seems Too Good to be True

We hear the warning all the time these days. "If a thing seems to be too good to be true then it probably is." Too often there is a report on the news or current affairs programs about someone having been "ripped off" by some con-man or person in another "get-rich-quick" scheme, or some poor person being left "out of pocket" because an unscrupulous tradesman has not delivered on unrealistic promises made. This warning is repeated.

Yet as I thought about this one night, I realized that there are some things that do seem to be too good to be true but *are* true. It seems too good to be true that a God who is perfect, made a perfect world and had it ruined by humans, didn't wipe them out and start all over again. Isn't it too good to be true that Jesus left His perfect Heaven to live on earth with sinful men, to show them how God wanted them to live? Why would anyone choose to die on an ugly cross, so that sinful people could have their sins forgiven? Simply because He loved them! Could anyone die, and come back to earth after three days in hell defeating Satan? Isn't that just too good to be true?

How could Jesus return to earth, and raise up those who believe in Him from the dead, even when they have been dead for years? How can a book be written and copied over and over again and yet remain an accurate translation of the original text?

If you come to Jesus and ask Him to show you the truth, then you will find that no matter how improbable these things may seem — YOU WILL FIND THAT THEY ARE TRUE!

74

Smog

As I discussed a situation with a fellow Christian, they expressed their wish that things were more black-and-white than they currently were. However, I don't think things can ever be black and white here on earth. We live between good and evil and therefore we live in, what can be called, a grey zone.

I thought about the parable of the Wheat and Tares, (Matthew 13:24-30). As a child I wondered why the farmer didn't make the workers go and pull up the weeds, wasn't it black and white? Wheat is clearly a wheat plant and thistles are clearly weeds. That was before I found out that tares are a weed that looks so much like wheat that it is very hard to tell the difference until they mature, and the seeds are set. Then I understood why the farmer requested that they be left alone until harvest. I think that he probably just shook his head in amazement at the arrogance of his staff. Did they really think that they could sort out the plants in their immature state?

We walk around in a spiritual smoggy world and the Bible tells us that the smog is going to get heavier as we get closer to Jesus' return. Despite this, we need to speak the truth in honest, simple terms, so that others will know what a wonderful God we have and how terrible hell will be, while we have time. There is only one way to move forward. That way is to take Jesus by the hand, in faith, and walk through the smog, doing what God wants us to, regardless of how grey things may look. After all, the hymn does say, "Stand up, Stand up for Jesus . . . . the battle will not be long."

75

Spiritual Diet

I have this problem with food. There are a lot of things that would either kill me or make me sick. So, I stick to a safe diet, which keeps me healthy, in order to not end up being housebound. On a recent trip away, it occurred to me that I was in danger of doing the same thing with my spiritual diet.

What is our spiritual diet? We are spiritually fed when meeting with other Christians. While reflecting on my childhood, I realised that we had contact with many Christians and learnt from them that God is a God of variety, that His arms are long and there is no way He can be put in a box. These days we have access to such a variety of Christian Speakers, but I isolate myself.

As God challenged me about this, I had to ask myself, why was I playing it safe? The answer was that I was getting lazy. If I want to try a new food, there is a process that needs to be carried out first. The ingredients checked very carefully and then after I actually eat it, I wait to make sure that there is no adverse reaction. Of course, if there is a reaction, then there's the process of dealing with that which has to be carried out and it's hard.

When we meet with other Christians and listen to other preachers, we need to make sure that what they are saying is Biblically correct. John tells us to "... but try the spirits whether they are of God: because many false prophets are gone out into the world." (1 John 4:1). Once I've done this, I'm happy to assume that it will remain safe, rather than bring vigilant; it's less work for me. Is God happy with me? Probably not?

76

Spoilt

Sometimes God spoils us so much. After a very sleepless night, my daughter and I had to rise early to get to a hospital appointment two hours away by 7 am. We arrived safely and I made contact with a friend for coffee, but she had to attend another meeting. I said that I would support her in prayer while I had my "cuppa". When I met her at 11.30, I asked how things had gone. She replied that she had had two positions filled despite only asking for one, something she had not expected.

Towards the end of our meal, I had a phone call from the hospital to say that my daughter was ready to go home, which was earlier than the expected 5 pm. When I collected her, I was told that not only had things gone very well but because she had worked so hard, carrying out the doctor's instructions over the previous month, she would not need the next operation. At the next visit, they would be able to go straight to the last operation and therefore complete a very long series of appointments and procedures.

As we were leaving the hospital, I listed several things I wanted to find. We were going to have a look at "Vinnies" (a second-hand store), and I suggested that it would be too much to ask for more miracles. Her reply was "Of course not". Our search produced everything we had listed.

Driving home I reflected on how many requests had been granted and marvelled at how sometimes God does give with full measure, pressed down and overflowing. James 4:6 tells how God is very gracious to those who are humble, and we were reminded that He sometimes surprises us with unexpected blessings that convince us of how much He loves us.

77

Targets

As my parents age, I find myself thinking more and more about how they have influenced my life. My father is a man who takes his role very seriously, some would say too seriously, but that is his way. He is a man who knows that people have to have an objective to aim for in life and for my sister and myself, that objective was given the day we were born. We were given our mothers' names. It was his desire that we would strive to be as Godly, modest, honest, and gracious as she was. While some of the message, for me at least, was lost in translation, I believe that the motivation was well-meant.

Paul talks about running the race of life and becoming like Christ in 1 Corinthians 9:24 and Philippians 3:13-14. I am not suggesting that we should worship humans. There is a difference between the worship of people and the realisation that they may be good examples to follow, particularly when they are people who have had a close relationship with God and therefore have developed those fruits of the spirit that Paul talks about in Galatians 5:22. Paul tells us in 1 Thessalonians 5:12, "But we beg you, brothers, to know those who labour among you, and are over you in the Lord, and admonish you."

Because we are human, messages are always going to have some loss in the translation, but the Holy Spirit is our translator and asking for assistance will ensure that we get the message that God wants us to hear. It may take longer to see it correctly, but God's ways are not our ways. The best example to follow of course is Christ, Himself. Ephesians 5:1 "Be imitators of God, therefore, as dearly loved children."

Who are you looking to?

78

The Big Picture

The picture shows a romantic shop/residence in spring with climbing roses on a lattice trellis out is full bloom, pots filled with various flowers, a large sign, bright red shutters on the windows, two large trees, bright clear blue sky, and gravelled parking area in the foreground. On the table there lay the 1000 pieces of the jigsaw that make up the completed picture on the box lid. Other members of the family had made a start. The border and the part of the house with the sign had nearly all the pieces together. I decided to help, and soon picked out the pieces that have parts of the shutters on them. While trying various pieces, finding that they don't fit and selecting others, my thoughts turn to how we often think about God's plan for history, is just like a jigsaw. As the windows and shutters are completed, work started on the areas that were much the same colour, such as the walls of the house, the blue sky, or the gravelled parking area.

Looking at the picture, I think about who would be represented by the pieces of the jigsaw. The brightly coloured, standout pieces to me would be people like David, John, Paul, Peter, Dorcas, the Wesley Brothers, Newton, and Spurgeon, great people of faith. While my part of the picture would be very difficult to find amongst the plain coloured pieces, I am exhilarated to realise, however, that the picture would never be completed if one piece (me) went missing.

Romans 12:4-6 reminds me that we are all part of the body of Christ, each with a different gift and therefore different roles to carry out. Do you know how important your role is, no matter how insignificant you think it is?

79

The Church—God's Family

God's principles don't change, just like God does not change, however, we do have to apply His principles in our modern world. How we do that *will* change. Change is something that comes more easily to some than others. Just like some people learn without effort, others must study for hours and hours just to pass.

God's principle for the church is that it is to be His family. Like every family, it has many branches spreading out all over the world. Each family has different requirements, likes, dislikes, traditions, and needs to be met in the community that they are part of. However, for a family to be a family, there has to be a relationship that is worked at or it will cease to exist. The most powerful tool that God has given us is communication. If we cannot communicate, either through words, touch, or body language then a relationship will finish.

If a family does not learn to communicate with love, forgiveness, respect, and cooperation, it becomes a dysfunctional family. God does not want that for us! King David's family was dysfunctional, and the Bible tells us how that turned out!

Every family will have its rebels or 'black sheep', but it is up to those that are left to make sure that the family is still able to relate to each other in a way that glorifies our Lord God. "By this shall all men know that ye are my disciples, if ye have love one to another." John 13:35. We need to show the world that even though we have different personalities and different levels of growth, we can still pull together. This will prove to the world that Jesus' love for them is real and that He wants them to have eternal life. (John 3:16).

80

The Daughter and the Gate

Years ago, there was a daughter who inherited a strong stubborn streak in her personality. One day at about the age of 2, the child decided that she could shut the gate after dad had left for work. Mum knew that the large gate needed to be lifted slightly to swing freely. So, they started off together, mum lifting slightly and daughter pushing, but then the daughter decided that things were going so well that she could do it all by herself and told her mother so in no uncertain terms. Mum let go, and the daughter discovered that the gate would no longer move when she pushed. The helpless look that she gave her mother told her that help was needed, but as soon as the gate was moving more freely, the child again decided that she was more than capable of shutting this gate on her own. Again, mum was told to let her do it by herself and again she found that the gate would not move with her strength alone. Eventually, the gate was closed, but not before there were several repeats of the above behaviour.

How like us is this child? We start off depending on God for our strength and when things seem to happen without a lot of effort then we push God into the background and try to move on in our own strength, only to find that things stall and then we have to stop and ask God to come back. We even promise that we will never shut Him out but then we fall into the same old trap of thinking that we are the ones doing the job, not God.

1 Corinthians 3:9 Paul reminds us "For we are labourers together with God: ye are God's husbandry, ye are God's building." He is the one that has the plans, strategies, means, and makes the opportunities for all the things that He needs done in order to have His plan fulfilled. What we need to do is make the choice to let Him use us, because if we don't, then He will use someone else to make things work and they will be the ones to receive the blessings that could have been ours.

If the daughter had just let her mother help her all the way from beginning to end there would have been the joy of a job well done. Instead, a job that should have taken one minute, took five and left two people feeling frustrated and exhausted.

81

The Parable of the Soils - Matthew 13:1-9

How often do we think about this parable as being a static parable? That is, do we believe that when God comes to sow the seed in people's hearts, they are a certain type of soil and will always be that type of soil? Are we inclined to think that God, the greatest farmer in existence, will only sow this ground once?

Many people, I fear, have had many sleepless nights worrying about which type of soil is in their hearts. Do we have concerns about the number of weeds in our lives and, therefore, believe that we cannot be good soil and bring forth fruit, some a hundredfold, some sixtyfold, some thirtyfold, as stated in scripture? Do we stereotype what fruit is? Do we declare that fruit is the conversion of people to Christianity?

God is an active farmer — a farmer who, time and time again, will plough the ground and dig the weeds. He picks the rocks up and makes use of them by making a wall, making a boundary for his people to stay within. It is a process that will last from the moment of birth to the moment of death. He never gives up and, while the good ground is busy producing all that fruit, let us remember that there will always be weeds in amongst the wheat, it just doesn't hinder the production process.

The parable does not tell us that the bad soil produces absolutely nothing either. What hinders its own production, will be used by God to enhance the soil of others, in much the same way as good gardeners use weeds for compost.

In this world bad choices, deep-seated attitudes, illness, or simply the evil that exists around us, that we absorb unwittingly, create stones, weeds, and thistles which reduce the production of good fruit. When God does the weeding, He shows us where we are going wrong. God is a loving farmer! He weeds gently, persistently, and will keep working on this paddock as long as the paddock exists. So, ground that was once very productive will have times when production is reduced, stony paths will not always be trodden on, thistles will not always choke out good seeds, but God will always tend His garden with love and care.

Our very definition of good fruit may be different to God's definition — it includes lessons that need to be learnt by those around us. Good fruit can be produced by meeting the challenges that the thorny ground produces and that production may not only be bringing souls into the kingdom but growth in the fruits of the spirit, Love, Joy, Peace, Longsuffering, Gentleness, Goodness, Faith, Meekness and Self-control. Read Galatians 5:22-23.

Do you believe that the greatest gardener can produce good fruit in you despite the kind of ground you believe you are?

82

The Snow Storm

While working in Glen Innes many years ago, during the winter I had to drive to Guyra several times a week. It was one of those winters with frequent snowfalls. During this time, I prayed "Lord, I have never ever driven in the snow before and I feel that I probably need to do it at least once in order to know if I am capable of managing such a challenge".

So of course, one night I started out and as I reached the mountains of Ben Lomond it started to snow. "Well here goes Lord you and I can do this" (I often talk to God like that when I'm driving) and on I went. At some point, I realised that I was in fact driving on the wrong side of the road and thanks to God's protection there had been no one coming the other way. When talking to a workmate several days later they indicated that ending up on the wrong side of the road was a very common consequence of driving in snow. It has something to do with the hypnotic effect of snow blowing across the road. Of course, when I realised that I was on the wrong side, I moved over and was even more careful. It took me longer to get to Guyra that night, but I arrived safely and can say that God and I met the Challenge.

In life as Christians, we are surrounded by sin all the time, it's in the airways and our natures, and sometimes we find ourselves on the wrong side of the road. Just like driving in the snow that night, when God has shown us the error of our ways, all we have to do is repent and with confidence remember Isaiah 44:22 "I (God) have blotted out, as a thick cloud, thy transgressions, and, as a cloud, thy sins: return unto me; for I have redeemed thee." We cannot avoid the challenge of living in a sinful world, but we can keep our eyes on Jesus and avoid ending up on the wrong side of the road.

83

The Story of the Three Wells

Its wintertime and our grandparents have come to stay. Sitting around the open fireplace one night we asked Grandma to tell us another one of her great stories. Mum wanted us in bed, and we were trying to put it off. "Ok", Grandma says "I'll tell you the story of the three wells. Well, well, well, now go to bed."

I am reminded of three different types of wells that I have heard about: the well that only fills very slowly after it is pumped out; the well that fills quickly and constantly and the well that a farmer looked into and found that it was dry. He shook his head, walked away not knowing what to do about it and as he did so, a rock fell off the side wall, allowing it to fill with water making it useful.

People are like these wells. There are those that have so many difficulties in their lives that they are limited in what they can give, others are being filled and filled and just pour out a labour for God that make us look on with awe, and then there are those that seem to be dry but after a life-changing event, it's as if God has pried away a rock blocking His life-giving water and they go from strength to strength. Each one is being used by God for His purpose and we must respect His plan for each one of us. "For as we have many members in one body, and all members have not the same office: So, we, being many, are one body in Christ, and every one members one of another. Having then gifts differing according to the grace that is given to us, whether prophecy, let us prophesy according to the proportion of faith;. . ." Romans 12:4-6

Like Grandma said, well, well, well, now get on with what God wants you to do.

84

The Unseen Guest

In our childhood home, we had a plaque that said, "Christ is the Head of this House, the silent listener to every conversation and the unseen Guest at every meal". Yes, he is the unseen presence everywhere, even here in church, and He knows each one of us through and through. He has made each one of us.

It always amazes me that God is the only person who can make so many things and not make any two the same. From the beginning of time until the end, He will have made each person that has ever lived, and they will not be a complete match to anyone else in existence. Just as Christ made you, Christ knows every cell you have, from the top of your head to the tip of your toes. He sees you better than any CT scan because a CT scan cannot tell how you feel but God knows, a CT scan cannot show anyone about your past feelings, or any secrets you may have, but God knows them all. A CT scan will not be able to predict how you will react to what others do or say, but God can, and a CT scan cannot show you what the future holds for you, but God can. He is the Alpha and the Omega, the beginning, and the end. Revelation 1:8

He is here today, and He wants you to open your heart to feel Him; open your ears to listen to Him, and open your mind to understand what He has in store for your future. However, there is just one thing that you must do for all this to happen and that is — you must be willing to allow Him to open your heart, ears, and mind.

85

Tough Times

A family I know were going through a time of uncertainty and they were naturally debating how God might or might not take them in several different directions. It's a debate that I'm sure all Christian families have had from time to time. During this time there were two verses that kept coming up. The first was "And we know that all things work together for good to them that love God, to them who are the called according to his purpose." Romans 8:28. The second was "As many as I love, I rebuke and chasten: be....." (Revelation 3:19). When thinking about one particularly tough possibility, one member commented: "God would not be that tough."

Thinking about this situation, I thought about how sad it is when people tell us that God will not allow us to go through tough times. Do they really believe that God does not love us and others enough to help us through these times? They are used to make us stronger, increase our knowledge, build our confidence, give us new skills, and practice skills we already have. They may also be about getting us to a place that we would not go otherwise, a place where God really wants us to be so that He can get His message of Salvation to someone who would not hear it otherwise. They may also help us get our priorities in a better order, which reminded me of a chorus from Sunday School called "JOY". It teaches children that we will have JOY if we put JESUS first, YOURSELF last, and OTHERS in between.

I have decided that some people are very self-motivated; others need to be led, with greater external force to get where God needs them. Either way, God's plan will not be foiled!

86

Turn on the Light

Have you ever found yourself with a problem that is not of your making, but one for which you could ultimately be held responsible? Well, recently I found myself in such a position. I went to bed one night, and as usual, turned out the light and tried to sleep. My mind did the turmoil thing — oh how it made mountains out of molehills, tore them down and rebuilt others in their place. Each mountain had very different consequences, which were greater than the one before. This went on for several hours, after which I declared, "Enough!" I turned on the light, resettled and strangely, dropped quickly off to sleep.

Morning arrived, and as I reflected on the night that was, I thought how sad it would be if I went to hell, where there is no light to turn on. In Matthew 22, we read the Parable of the Marriage Feast, in which those that have not followed the Lord, will be cast into outer darkness and there will be weeping and gnashing of teeth. (Verse 13). As there is no light to turn on and divert my thought patterns, it will go on forever. How sad for anyone who chooses to ignore the call of God and end up in hell.

John 1: 7-9 declares that Jesus is the light of the world, showing us the way to Heaven. "Jesus saith unto him, I am the way, the truth, and the life: no man cometh unto the Father, but by me." (John 14:6).

We are not responsible for the choices people make about God, but we are responsible for making sure that they know there is a choice to be made, and that Jesus will offer them a way out of eternal darkness.

87

Ugly Beauty

We have this section of garden which has been known to harbour the odd snake and, when I checked it out, I discovered that there was so much dead wood and grass around that I decided to turn this ugly patch into a thing of beauty. So, I cautiously started raking, cutting, pulling, and pruning but it was not long before I lost count of the number of times that I had said "Oops, I shouldn't have done that!" as healthy parts of the plants were destroyed. I gave thanks again that God is so much better at pruning our lives and the church than I was at pruning these plants. After about a week, I decided that in order not to inflict any more havoc, it was time to enjoy its ugliness and just feed and water the garden so that the plants had a chance to grow stronger and healthier.

I wondered how much damage we inflict on others when we try to judge and enforce our ideas and discipline on those within our churches. Some churches have members with very visible scars from abuse or mental illness and yet, as they are fed, these members grow slowly in the love of God. For people who are not very strong, irreparable damage can be done in the eagerness to create what we think is a beautiful church.

Three times Jesus instructed Peter to "Feed My sheep," (John 21:15-17) He did not say "Feed My sheep, Drench My sheep, Shear My sheep." It is so easy to add more to what God has to say. Yes, our churches and lives are cluttered with ugly sins — selfishness, pride, apathy. Let us just get on with feeding people in the church and leave the beautification to God, regardless of how we see things.

88

Under Attack

"Sleep, wonderful sleep, I hope that it comes quickly," I think as I pull the covers up and settle down for what, I hope, is a good night's rest as I am feeling worn out. No sooner is the light out and the covers up than I hear a familiar whining sound. A mosquito!! "That would be right," I think "just like the devil, it decides to wait until its dark to attack me." (John 3:19b) "Men loved darkness instead of light, because their deeds were evil." I wave my arms in a vain attempt to fight back and kill it, but of course, that does not work, it is far too fast and it's dark so I can't see it to actually hit it anyway. So the attacks keep on happening. In the end, I decide the only way to defend myself is to pull the covers over my head and rely on their protection. As I settle down again, it occurs to me, thankfully, that Jesus offers much better protection against the devil than my blankets do against that mosquito.

"Finally, my brethren, be strong in the Lord, and in the power of his might. Put on the whole armour of God, that ye may be able to stand against the wiles of the devil. For we wrestle not against flesh and blood, but against principalities, against powers, against the rulers of the darkness of this world, against spiritual wickedness in high places. Wherefore take unto you the whole armour of God, that ye may be able to withstand in the evil day, and having done all, to stand. Stand therefore, having your loins girt about with truth, and having on the breastplate of righteousness; And your feet shod with the preparation of the gospel of peace; Above all, taking the shield of faith, wherewith ye shall be able to quench all the fiery darts of the wicked. And take the helmet of salvation, and the sword of the Spirit, which is the word of God:" Ephesians 6:10-17.

Are you wearing the armour of God?

89

Unexpected Teachers

Encouragement is such a difficult thing to do. So often we try to encourage our children and are surprised when we discover that they have taken our words and/or actions the wrong way. How we would like people to be born with operating manuals (like the new washing machine)? Any set of parents could have a hundred children and they would all be different. A few years ago, we discovered that one of our children has a very mixed up human body with organs back to front and the wrong way around etc. I went on a guilt trip over someone's comments on how I had not been helpful in the development of their crazy makeup. That child was the one to put me in my place, "But they should have known better than to say that" the child said. "You had nothing to do with it, God put me together the way I am for whatever reasons He had — not you." So often we are lifted and inspired more when encouragement comes from an unexpected source.

In 1 Timothy 4:12 Paul says, "Let no man despise thy youth; but be thou an example of the believers, in word, in conversation, in charity, in spirit, in faith, in purity." And yes, there are times when the older generations have the opportunity to learn from the younger Christians around us.

1 Timothy 5:1-2 "Rebuke not an elder, but entreat him as a father; and the younger men as brethren; The elder women as mothers; the younger as sisters, with all purity." If we do these things, we will learn from each other. In Colossians 4:6 it says "Let your speech be always with grace.. . ."

I wonder who God will use today to teach us something and surprise us?

90

Waiting

There was a ripple of laughter as the children upstaged the minister with the wrong answer to his question during the children's talk. Things were not going according to plan! Listening to the laughter, I think, what a pity I cannot have the same sense of humour when my own plans going astray. It is again a situation when I need to say, "not as I will, but as you will." Matthew 26:39b

Stepping out in faith is one thing but learning to wait in faith is another. It looks as if God is taking me in a direction that is completely different to where I would like to go. I need to wait and see what God's will is. When you are a person of action, it is extremely hard to wait, and I don't like standing still.

Oh yes, I have rebuked myself with the usual platitudes, "For my thoughts are not your thoughts, neither are your ways my ways, declares the Lord." (Isaiah 55:8) and "We know that in all things God works for the good of those who love him, who have been called according to His purpose." Romans 8:28. But my heart wants to get up and get going!

I am reminding myself of how good God has been to me in the past and this is helping me to trust Him with a little less fear and trembling, but I am also dismayed at how badly I manage to be an imitator of Christ. Hebrews 13:7 "Remember them which have the rule over you, who have spoken unto you the word of God: whose faith follow, considering the end of their conversation."

So, I have to learn to sit in faith and see what the Lord will do. What about you?

91

What Faith?

During a discussion with a colleague about our need for rain, and my need to get some jobs done before it came, I was asked if I expected enough rainfall to make the roads impassable. My response was 'no', but there is no point asking for rain and not being ready when it comes.

While reflecting on this conversation, it occurred to me that often we ask God for things, not really believing that God will answer or give what we ask for. It's a bit like the story I heard as a child, of an American congregation that held a special prayer meeting for rain during a drought, but the only member to turn up carrying an umbrella was an eight-year-old child.

If we want God to answer our prayers then it makes sense to act as if He will. Years ago, when our house became too small for our growing family, I asked God to help us find a larger home. Some friends came around to visit a few days later to find me packing our excess goods. "What's going on?" they asked, and the response was "Well I asked God for a larger house, so I have started packing to be ready to move when we find it."

God answered my prayer two years later and yes, I had to manoeuvre around packed boxes for the two years, but I was still ready when God answered.

Hebrews 11:6 "But without faith it is impossible to please him: for he that cometh to God must believe that he is, and that he is a rewarder of them that diligently seek him."

92

What Is?

What is in a gift? Pastor, preacher, evangelist, or teacher they are all very important and they are only different in the way that they communicate with another person. A pastor, for instance, feels more comfortable in small groups and can relate to people—feel their pain and most importantly help them know that God cares for them.

A preacher talks to many people at once and has the ability to explain the gospel and what God wants from all of us. An evangelist stirs the emotions of his hearers and seeks decisions, while a teacher tells his hearers the Gospel more in story form, showing that God has an eternal plan.

What the gift is, does not matter. It's what the message is that's important, and that the message is not watered down regardless of who delivers it.

What is the message?—John 3:16 tells us "For God so loved the world, that he gave his only begotten Son, that whosoever believeth in him should not perish, but have everlasting life.." 1 Corinthians 13:1 also tells us that it does not matter who delivers the message. If we do not have love then we may as well be a clanging gong.

God has given each of us a gift and a group of people to minister to. If we look at others and think that they will be able to reach people better or do a better job than us, aren't we in danger of telling God that He has made a mistake. Something we all know God does not do!

93

What is a Mission Field?

I once heard of a missionary working for many years in the field and only managing to lead one native to Christianity. Yet, even though he considered himself to be a failure, he is now considered by others to have been faithful in his service to the Lord, as that one native led others to Christ. It is easy for us to think of countries overseas as mission fields because it means someone leaving home and being very lonely with very little support. We should, in this day and age, be looking a lot closer to home.

As I look around our services lately, I see many faces missing, and I have heard that they are fellowshipping elsewhere because, it would seem, that they are not happy with our church. I know that God will call people to new mission fields from time to time, but I wonder if they are not ignoring a call to the toughest mission field ever — home.

God does not call us to be faithful only in good times but calls us to be faithful no matter what he calls us to do. (Revelation 2:10). I get the feeling that some people see church in the western world as a club with a refreshment bar, not a mission field. While ever there are people in our society, here at home, who do not know and love our Lord Jesus Christ and are going to hell because they have ignored His call, then our church is our mission field. It does not matter if you and one other person are the only people who are faithfully serving Him, because "for where two or three come together in my name there I am with them." Matthew 18:20.

Where is your mission field?

94

What Privacy?

Someone once commented that there was no privacy in the city. Yes, that is true, particularly if the blinds are open, but this exposure can bring an accountability that would not be felt by a hermit. Right or wrong, as strangers pass your garden you will be judged — that secret judgement you may never know about and they may be wrong, but it is still passed.

Being aware that judgements will be made can spur some of us on to accomplish higher levels of achievements than we might otherwise rise to. Do we remember, however, that our lives are completely exposed to God every day and every night? Psalm 139 tells us that God has searched us and knows everything about us (Verse 1) and if we try and run away and hide from Him, He will always be able to find us — Verse 11 & 12 "If I say, Surely the darkness shall cover me; even the night shall be light about me. Yea, the darkness hideth not from thee; but the night shineth as the day: the darkness and the light are both alike to thee."

We may think that we have privacy, something that people seem to want more of today; but God sees us and loves us and wants us to let Him help us achieve those standards that He has set for us. Let us remember though there is a word of warning in the bible, which tells us that one day there will be judgement and if we have not accepted that gift of love that Jesus gave to us we will run out of chances. Just as man is destined to die once, and after that to face judgment (Heb 9: 27).

95

Who will Go?

Many years ago, our eight or nine-year-old granddaughter came to stay, and she was asked to go and make her bed. Her reply was, "But I know how to make my bed." As far as she was concerned even though she could do something, it was still someone else's responsibility — in this case, mine.

A few years later my granddaughter's younger sister came to stay when she was about the same age. Each morning as I walked past her room — her bed was made — no fuss, just done and it made my world a better place to be.

Some Christians, I fear, fall into this same trap. They pray for God to save their neighbour's soul, or bring His love to those overseas, or teach their children of His love, but that's as far as their responsibility goes. God is responsible for making it all happen and they are happy to sit at the foot of the cross and pray.

In Isaiah 6:8 God asks, Who shall I send, who will go for us? and Isaiah's response is, "Here am I. Send me!" and we have the record of what he did. While we may not be called to the massive undertakings of Isaiah, Moses, Jeremiah, or even David, we are called to do something each day which will spread God's word a little further, and make our world a better place to be.

96

Why I won't ask for Healing

I am diabetic. This illness is not life-threatening but definitely very inconvenient. It has been suggested to me by others that I should ask God for complete healing. When God says that all things work together for the good of those who love Him and are called according to His purpose (Romans 8:28) — I have to believe that this includes my illness. Don't get me wrong, I know that God could heal me if He wanted to and He may choose to heal others, if they ask, but I have already seen so much good come from having this problem, that I am content with just keeping it under control.

This has allowed me to regain my courage and fire for ministry and has also made me aware that now is the time to get things done, despite the hurdles in my way, rather than wait for some other, easier, time. God has helped me to develop a level of self-control that I did not have before. That has enabled me to keep this monster well tethered so far. Yes, I still have days when it would be easier to let go and there are still days when I ask God what His purpose is. I know even then, in my head, that He has a plan for me, a good and gracious plan (Philippians 2:13) "for it is God who works in you to will and to act according to His good pleasure." And at the end of the age, I want to be there when He calls my name. In the meantime, I am doing what I can to keep this problem controlled. I am waiting to see what else God may want to accomplish through me while I have diabetes, rather than removing it and making my life less inconvenient.

97

Works

In another time and another place, I was Superintendent of a growing Sunday School, attached to a static church. It became necessary to get some extra helpers, and after several requests to the church members, one member came to me and said, "I'm praying that you will get the help you need". I nodded and said, "thank you", but my heart cried to God "I wish people would get off their knees and pray on their feet". In other words, get up and do something. I have used and heard a lot of excuses for not taking part in church ministries: "I don't like that", "I'm not good at that", "I'm too busy", "It's not my thing", to name just a few.

I'm reminded about what the bible says in James 2 about faith and works, and verse 20 declares that . . ."faith without works is dead." For instance, faith that a chair will not collapse if you sit on it does not work unless you actually sit down.

If God is prompting you to assist in any ministries such as Bible Study, Chaplaincy, Crèche, Church Maintenance, Committee of Management, Mentoring, Play Group, Prayers on Wheels, Women's Ministries, Scripture, Service Leading, Sunday School, Visitation, WOW, or Youth Group then maybe it's time to put the excuses aside and step up. Are you resisting God's desire for you to help somewhere in your church? Then take 2 Corinthians 12:9 "My grace is sufficient for you, for my strength is made perfect in weakness." it's time to roll up our sleeves and move those feet.

I'm not suggesting that people do something that God doesn't want them to do but sometimes I think we often say "NO," without even asking God when it is suggested that some ministry could use our help.

98

Worship

Worship. What does it mean? I was thinking about what this word means and found that for me worship has three parts to it.

Firstly, I have to come and ask forgiveness for my sins, aware of how great our God is and how much He hates sin. Psalm 139:23-24 "Search me, O God, and know my heart: try me, and know my thoughts: And see if there be any wicked way in me, and lead me in the way everlasting."

Secondly, I come to praise Him with all the thankfulness that I am able to find, for life, good or bad, for the freedom to come into church, for food to eat, friends, and family. Regardless of how happy or dysfunctional they are, they are still family and there are others that have none of these things. Ephesians 5:20 says "Giving thanks always for all things unto God and the Father in the name of our Lord Jesus Christ."

Thirdly, I come to learn the lessons that God has for me; not the person next to me, not the person that has hurt me, or the person that I don't like, but the lesson for me. God loves me as an individual and He has a message that will fit my circumstances, my learning style, my needs, and stage of life. Psalm 25:4 says: "Shew me thy ways, O Lord; teach me thy paths."

How will you Worship today?

99

Wise Men Seek God

Many years ago, I heard a Christmas sermon titled "Wise Men Seek God". In summary, it said that there were three groups of people involved in the birth of Christ and compared them to groups of people today. Firstly, the general population of Jerusalem, who were really quite unaware of Jesus' existence. Many people today are just as unaware. Secondly, there were those who were out to actively kill Jesus. At His birth, this was, of course, Herod, but today they would be those who persecute Christians all over the world. The person delivering this sermon felt that this is fairly uncommon in our time. The third group was the Wise Men. These were those that searched for Christ and, while it was not directly stated, it was implied that these people went to Heaven.

Now, I'm a picky person. On the way home, my daughter and I just had to rewrite this one. Yes, we agreed that a large percentage of the population have no idea of God's existence, let alone the existence of Jesus. However, try and tell the people of the Sudan and South Africa that there were very few people out there actively seeking to persecute the Christian Church. It is noted here that there has been an increase in oppression since then. Next, we came to the third group, the Wise Men. Don't people realise that, while it is less likely to happen today, many churches have people that seek God each Sunday and then go home, just like those wise men? On Monday morning many worshippers would not give Christianity any credit by the way they carry out their business, or the by the way they behave.

What was missing from this sermon? The fourth group! Mary and Joseph, representing those people who have a day to day relationship with Jesus and who are part of His family. They are the people who will go to Heaven. Titus 3:7 states, "That being justified by his grace, we should be made heirs according to the hope of eternal life." This is what God sent Jesus for and while seeking Him out is good, it is not enough. We must stay and become part of His family to obtain the gift of eternal life. Are you part of Jesus' family or still seeking?

100

Writers Block

Suffering from writer's block is frustrating. I seemed to be completely uninspired for a period of a few weeks. Questions that ran through my empty head were things like — Why? Am I focused on the wrong things around me? Have I taken my eyes off Jesus? But the biggest one was: how do ministers get through periods like this? In spite of everything, they have no choice; they have to come up with something every week! What would we say if our minister stood in the pulpit one Sunday and announced that he had no sermon, God had not given him one for that week? Would someone out of the congregation stand up and say, "that's alright I have a sermon to share" or would we all sit in stunned silence. I suspect the latter.

After all, all I have had to do is put three hundred words together to be used occasionally. Ministers have to come up with one or more sermons a week, put bible studies together, visit the sick and parishioners, help and counsel those in need, decipher new regulations, attend meetings and conduct funerals to list just a few before they try to find time for themselves and their families.

Do we take for it granted that all our ministers and church leaders will deliver each week, or do we continually pray for them and do what Paul requests of us in 1 Thessalonians 5:12-13 "And we beseech you, brethren, to know them which labour among you, and are over you in the Lord, and admonish you; And to esteem them very highly in love for their work's sake. And be at peace among yourselves"

Do you pray for those in leadership in your church?

Other Books by this Author
All these books are available as eBooks

More Water into Wine, 2nd Edition
100 Stories of God's Hand in Life

Reflections
Australian Stories from my Father's Past

365 Glasses of Wine
Short Devotionals for each day of the year

Conversations with Myself – Volume 1
100 Stories of Hope, Faith and Determination

Still More Water into Wine
100 Stories of God's Hand in Life

Whispers from on High
Poetry and short stories.

Follow Helen Brown on:
Facebook: https://www.facebook.com/HelenBrownCollection/

Instagram: https://www.instagram.com/helen_brown_books/

Pinterest: https://www.pinterest.com.au/helenbrown58726/

www.ingramcontent.com/pod-product-compliance
Lightning Source LLC
Chambersburg PA
CBHW030301010526
44107CB00053B/1776